IMAGES
of America

ALLEGHENY CITY
1840–1907

IMAGES
of America

ALLEGHENY CITY
1840–1907

The Allegheny City Society

ARCADIA
PUBLISHING

Published by Arcadia Publishing
Charleston, South Carolina

Library of Congress Catalog Card Number: 2007927944

For all general information contact Arcadia Publishing at:
Telephone 843-853-2070
Fax 843-853-0044
E-mail sales@arcadiapublishing.com
For customer service and orders:
Toll-Free 1-888-313-2665

Visit us on the Internet at www.arcadiapublishing.com

CONTENTS

ACKNOWLEDGMENTS

The Allegheny City Society is an organization whose mission is preserving the history of that portion of the city of Pittsburgh known prior to December 1907 as Allegheny City. That date, and the desire to recognize (not necessarily celebrate) this annexation, has spurred the society to create this book that captures many of the images of the people, buildings, and environment that made up our "lost" city.

Ruth McCartan (committee chair), John and Ann Canning, Michael and Eleanor Coleman, David Grinnell, John Makar, Michael Shealey, and Lois Yoedt spent many hours pouring through the society's archives selecting, scanning, documenting, and organizing the images that were eventually chosen for publication. Without their efforts, this book would have remained a "future project."

To supplement the society's and committee members' archives, many individuals have contributed images and photographs from their family collections: Darlane Abel, Jeffery Bees, Janet Fazio, Ed Hahn, Richard Lerach, Doug Lucas, Peg MacCall, Suzanne Maury, Terry Mowrey, Don Walter, Mary Wohleber, and Timothy Zinn.

Other images and information were made available by the Carnegie Library of Pittsburgh, the Senator John Heinz History Center, the Little Sisters of the Poor, the University of Pittsburgh's Archives of Industrial Society, and the Pittsburgh History and Landmarks Foundation.

—Mike Coleman, President, Allegheny City Society

INTRODUCTION

In the opening years of the 19th century, Allegheny Town was but a small collection of families living in log houses along the north bank of the Allegheny River. Across the river was the more populous frontier village of Pittsburgh. Within the span of a century, both communities would grow in size and significance. By the year 1900, Allegheny City was the third-largest city, population wise, in the state of Pennsylvania. The transformation of Allegheny from a wilderness hamlet to one of America's major industrial cities is a fascinating story. Each decade of the century witnessed population growth, economic expansion, and a growing sense of civic pride.

As with all communities, there were a number of key players in Allegheny's story, and they came with different perspectives of what contributed to the common good. In most cases they tended to complement one another's vision. Mayors and town councilors such as William Robinson, Hezekiah Nixon, Lewis Peterson Jr., Ormsby Phillips, and David B. Oliver spearheaded programs and institutions that improved the quality of life for the city's residents.

Religious leaders, including Joseph Stockton, John Stibiel, Carl Weiterhausen, and James M. Fulton, not only gathered religious congregations but founded schools and institutions to address the physical as well as the spiritual needs of Alleghenians.

Many times it was the compassion and determination of Allegheny's women such as Dr. Jane Vincent, Mary H. Brunot, Rachel McFadden, Louise Lyle, and Kate McKnight who focused the eyes of the community on the plight of orphans, the sick, the aged, and the poor that lived in all the neighborhoods of the city.

Industrialists and business leaders such as Andrew Carnegie, B. F. Jones, Theodore H. Nevin, and Henry J. Heinz were but a few of Allegheny's entrepreneurs who contributed to the economic development and expansion of the entire region, providing jobs for waves of immigrants who settled in Allegheny communities throughout the century.

In the field of science and technology, the likes of John Brashear and Samuel P. Langley are definitely two shining stars, and in the arts, the names of George Hetzel, Martha Graham, Mary Cassatt, and Mary Roberts Rinehart are but a few artists with roots in Allegheny City.

In the years between 1840, when Allegheny Town was incorporated as a city, and 1890, when Alleghenians celebrated the city's 50th anniversary, Allegheny City had greatly grown in population. The area of the city had more than tripled in size through the friendly annexation of surrounding municipalities.

Allegheny City's story followed a classic pattern of American urban history, one characterized by dynamism, optimism, and expansionism. On December 7, 1907, that story came to an abrupt end when Allegheny City ceased to exist and became known as the North Side of Pittsburgh. The story of Pittsburgh's North Side is for others to tell.

ALLEGHENY COMMEMORATIVE METAL. The celebration of the 50th anniversary of Allegheny City's incorporation as a city occurred in 1890. Residents and organizations of the city celebrated their community's history throughout the year. A medal was cast, which incorporated the city's seal, to commemorate this glorious event. The last decade of the 19th century was an exceptional period in Allegheny City's history. The Allegheny Post Office was constructed nearby the town center. Hay Market Square was transformed into the exquisite Diamond Park. Over 200 acres of former farmland at the north end of the city became the city's Riverview Park, which boasted Allegheny's own zoo. Technological advances in bridge building and electrically powered trolley systems opened the areas along Perrysville and California Avenues as well as Brighton Road into Allegheny's "streetcar suburbs." Alleghenians at the end of the 1890s, the fin de siècle, were filled with a strong sense of civic pride based on the accomplishments of the previous 50 years. The commemorative medal signified the depth and extent of Alleghenians' identity with their city.

One

ALLEGHENY TOWN

TOWN HALL. Allegheny Town was established by order of the executive council of Pennsylvania in 1787 as a village in a 3,000-acre tract of wilderness opposite Pittsburgh. By 1828, the population of the hamlet had grown to 4,000 residents, and the town was incorporated as a borough. The town hall of the borough of Allegheny was constructed in 1834 at the intersection of Ohio and Federal Streets. Until it was replaced in 1864, the town hall served both as a municipal center and a public safety building.

OHIO

RIVER

ALL

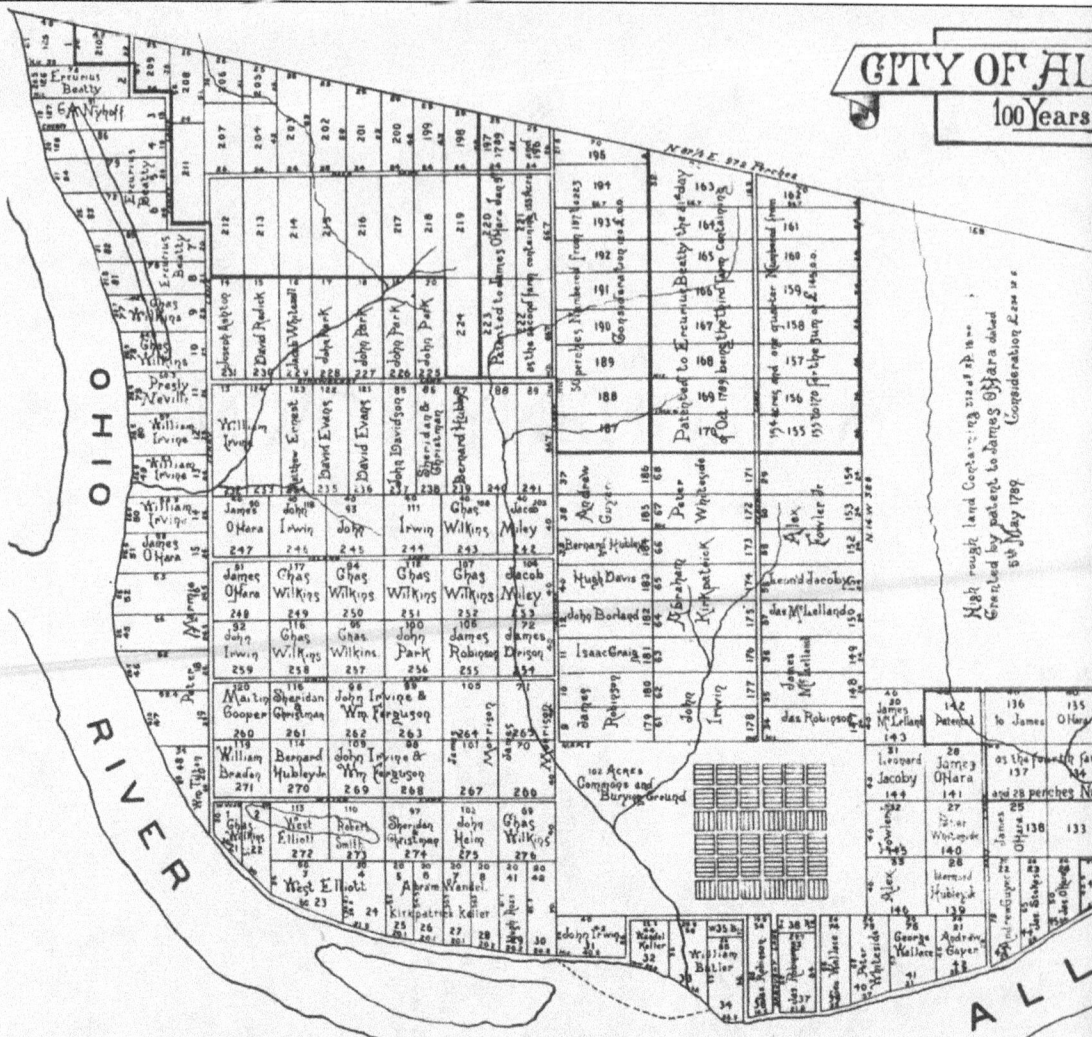

Note The Town Lots are numbered with black and the Out-lots with red ink and reciprocally refer from one to the other.
The remaining Out-lots are laid out into Farms, as delineated by the red lines.
I do certify that the above is a copy of the original remaining in the Surveyor Generals Office of Pennsylvania.
In Testimony whereof I have hereto set my hand and affixed the seal of said Office at Harrisburgh the 2nd day of October A.D. 1849.
For John Laporte S.G.
R.M. Crem

MAP OF
RESERVE TRACT OF LAND
OPPOSITE PITTSBURH.
Surveyed by Daniel Leet.

TOWN OF ALLEGANY

NORTH

WEST

STREET

STREET

STREET

STREET

OHIO   STREET

BEAVER   FEDERAL   SANDUSKY

OUT LOTS RED   SOUTH   TOWN LOTS BLACK

LEET'S MAP OF THE TRACT OPPOSITE PITTSBURGH. State-appointed surveyors divided the 3,000-acre "Reserve Tract opposite Pittsburgh" into 276 "out-lots," each containing about 10 acres of land. In the center of the tract, north of the floodplain, a plan of 128 "inlots" was identified as the Allegheny Town center. Four squares were set aside in the very center of the town for public use. The town center was surrounded by over 100 acres of common land. Proceeds from the sale of the entire tract were used by the state government to offset the state's debt to the troops who served in the war for American independence.

11

JAMES O'HARA. This Irish-born Revolutionary War veteran and prominent resident of Pittsburgh purchased more land in the reserved tract than any other individual. James O'Hara's descendants, the Denny, Paxton, McKnight, Brereton, Darlington, and Schenley families, were major property owners and developers throughout the 19th century.

James O'Hara

KILBUCK. The Kilbuck estate, located along Western Avenue, was built around 1823 by the rector of Trinity Episcopal Church in Pittsburgh. The name Kilbuck was based on the belief that the Native American chief Kilbuck was buried in the garden area of the estate. Around 1840, the property was given as a wedding gift to Robert and Elizabeth Denny McKnight by the bride's parents, James and Elizabeth O'Hara Denny.

WILLIAM ROBINSON. The only son of James and Martha Boggs Robinson, William Robinson was born in 1785. James operated an inn and a ferry connecting Franklin Road (Federal) in Allegheny Town with St. Clair Street (Sixth) in Pittsburgh. William inherited considerable property throughout Allegheny. He took a leading role in the transformation of Allegheny from a frontier village to a robust city and was elected the first mayor in 1840.

ROBINSON HOMESTEAD. As Allegheny Town grew in size and significance, so did the family of William and Mary Parker Robinson. To accommodate a family of 10 children, the Robinsons built a large home at the north end of the St. Clair (Sixth) Street Bridge. William took a leading role in the development of this bridge, which was opened in 1820. William died in this home in 1868.

REV. JOSEPH STOCKTON. In the early 1800s, Allegheny Town, a frontier hamlet, had a growing number of families with roots in Scotland and the Ulster section of Ireland. In 1812, Rev. Joseph Stockton, a Presbyterian pastor, began preaching to this community in an open-air setting in the western part of the commons. From these beginnings, Stockton gathered together the congregation of the First Presbyterian Church of Allegheny Town.

FIRST PRESBYTERIAN CHURCH. Stockton guided this congregation of Presbyterians as it built its first church structure in the commons just west of Stockton Avenue. Following a conflict over the use of the commons, the leaders of this Presbyterian congregation decided to locate their second church building, shown here, on Beaver Street (Arch Street) that was in the town and not the commons.

THOMAS BARLOW HOUSE. This home of Thomas and Anica Preble Barlow was drawn from sketches made by Anica and sent to a friend in France. Anica, educated in a prestigious girls' school in France, was a friend of the Marquis de Lafayette. During the French hero's last visit to the United States in 1825, the Barlows hosted a reception for him in their home at the base of Hogsback (Monument) Hill.

HARRIET PREBLE. A French-educated woman, Harriet Preble immigrated to America in 1830 to live near her sister, Anica Preble Barlow. Both sisters established schools for girls. Aside from their homes in Allegheny, the Barlows and Prebles had "summer seats" across from Brunot's Island in the tiny village of Manchester. Harriet and Anica had considerable impact on the young women who attended their schools and later became significant leaders in Allegheny's history.

FIRST ASSOCIATE REFORMED PRESBYTERIAN CHURCH. In 1831, the congregation of the First Associate Reformed Presbyterian Church of Allegheny was gathered. Issues of theology and polity in Scotland and Ireland contributed to this denomination being separate from the "main line" Presbyterians. This congregation played a pivotal role in the establishment of the Pittsburgh Seminary and was the mother church of many congregations in Allegheny.

REV. DR. JOHN TAYLOR PRESSLY. Rev. Dr. John Taylor Pressly was the dynamic first pastor of the First Associate Reformed Presbyterian Church of Allegheny (after 1858 the denomination was known as the United Presbyterian Church of North America). Pressly led this congregation from 1833 to 1870. He was instrumental in the organization of the denomination's seminary in Allegheny as well as in the gathering of new congregations.

MARIA RICKENBACH VOEGTLY. A large contingent of the Rickenbach and Voegtly families, including Maria Rickenbach Voegtly, emigrated from Switzerland to Allegheny Town in 1823. Heinrich Rickenbach Sr., Maria's father, and Nicholas Voegtly, her father-in-law, purchased 22 out-lots from the James O'Hara estate. This property was along the bank of the Allegheny River on the eastern part of the reserve tract. This community later became known as Allegheny's Dutchtown.

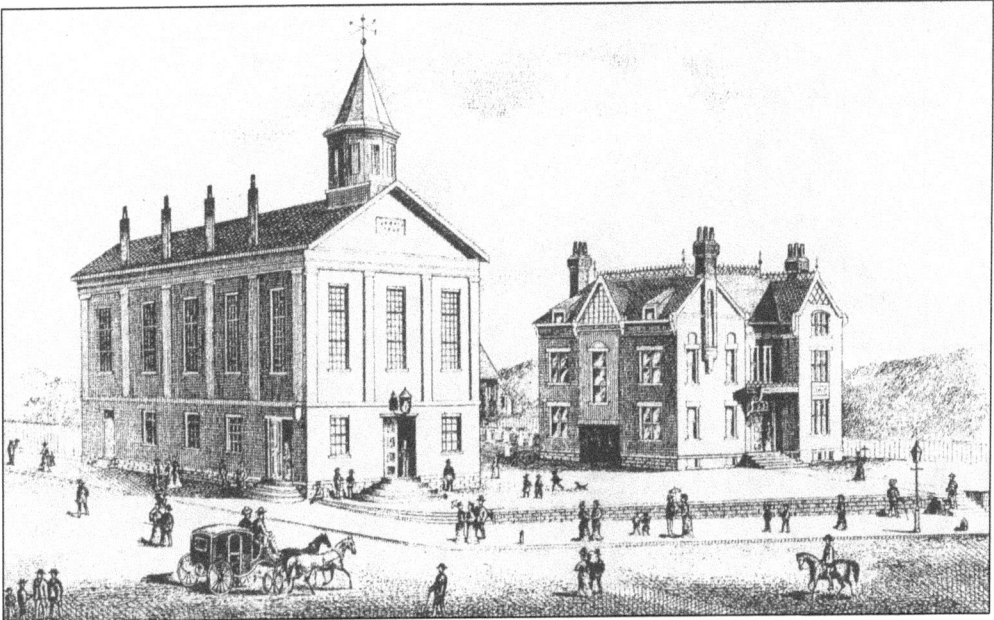

VOEGTLY CHURCH. The German Evangelical Protestant Church of Allegheny Town was founded in 1833 as a place of worship for the growing community of German-speaking settlers in Allegheny. Members of the Voegtly family gave the property where the church was built, as well as much of the funding for its construction and operation. It was often referred to as "the Voegtly Church."

REV. CARL WEITERHAUSEN. From 1839 until 1846, Rev. Carl Weiterhausen pastored the young congregation of the Voegtly Church. Weiterhausen was an enthusiastic preacher, and under his leadership, the congregation grew in membership and influence. However, issues arose within the congregation between the pastor and the church lay leaders. This resulted in Weiterhausen and a group of his followers leaving the Voegtly Church in 1846.

WEITERHAUSEN CHURCH. Those members who followed Weiterhausen after he left the Voegtly Church formed a new congregation known as the German Evangelical Protestant Church of St. Paul's congregation. They purchased land along the south side of the Pennsylvania Canal where their first church building was constructed in 1847. Weiterhausen served this congregation until 1868. The church was often called the "Weiterhausen Church."

WESTERN THEOLOGICAL SEMINARY. In 1825, the general assembly of the Presbyterian Church authorized the founding of a theological seminary west of the Appalachians. Allegheny Town was selected as the site for the seminary. Pastor Joseph Stockton of the First Presbyterian Church of Allegheny Town was active in the establishment of the Western Theological Seminary. The seminary building pictured here opened in 1831. It was located on Hogsback (Seminary or Monument) Hill.

WESTERN PENITENTIARY. Allegheny Town was designated by the state government in 1818 as the location of a new state prison. The land on which the prison was to be built was identified in the legislation as 10 acres of the common land surrounding the town center. The construction of the Western Penitentiary, designed to look like a medieval fortress, was completed in 1825. It remained in the commons until 1886.

CHARLES AVERY. Charles Avery was one of the leaders of Allegheny's flourishing cotton-milling industries before the Civil War. As an enterprising businessman, Avery invested in a number of ventures and amassed a considerable fortune in the copper-mining industry. A leader within the Methodist Protestant denomination and a staunch abolitionist, Avery donated very generously to causes designed to end slavery and improve conditions for the African American community.

AVERY INSTITUTE AND THE AVERY AFRICAN METHODIST EPISCOPAL CHURCH. Charles Avery's estate was located not far from the cotton mills in Allegheny's Fourth Ward. On these grounds Avery founded and generously supported the Avery College, a school for the education of African American teachers as well as a preparatory school for African American youngsters in the region. From this institute emerged the congregation of the Avery African Methodist Episcopal Zion congregation.

PROTESTANT ORPHANS HOME.
As the population of Allegheny Town increased in the 1820s, an awareness of children without parental support caused a group of citizens to establish an orphanage. The Protestant Orphan Asylum of Pittsburgh and Allegheny was incorporated in 1834. William Robinson donated $7,500 and land on Webster (Sherman) Avenue as a site for the building designed by architect John Chislett. The building was opened in 1836.

FIRE DEPARTMENT. One of the first acts of the elected leaders of the borough of Allegheny was to address the concern of fire protection in the community. In 1829, two fire engines were purchased and then a more powerful engine in 1833. By 1840, when the borough of Allegheny became Allegheny City, there were four fire companies located at different sites in the community.

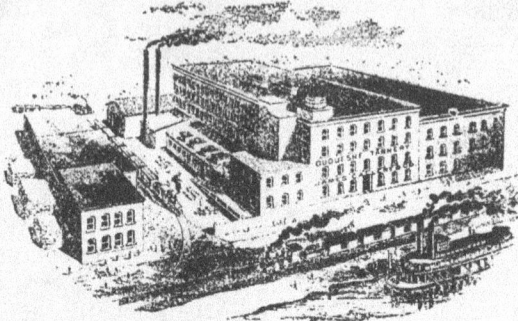

JAMES CALLERY & CO.
Leather Manufacturers.

OAK

HARNESS

SHOE

GRAINS

UNION

HARNESS

FINISHED

SPLITS

DUQUESNE TANNERY.

DUQUESNE TANNERY. Economic development in Allegheny in the first quarter of the 19th century led to the establishment of a number of new businesses. A by-product of the meatpacking industry was the leather business. James Callery was one of the pioneers in Allegheny's tanning community. Callery's firm, the Duquesne Tannery, was located on River Road on the north bank of the Allegheny River.

Pioneer Paint Works.
Established 1841.

Pittsburgh, Jan 15th 1873

Mr. J. F. Dias

Bought of **T. H. Nevin & Co.**

OFFICE — N.W. Cor. of 34 Ave. & Market St

THEODORE H. NEVIN'S PIONEER PAINT WORKS. Companies producing white lead-based paint were organized in Allegheny as early as 1831. Theodore H. Nevin's firm that was advertised as Pioneer Paint Works was founded in 1841. It had plants at Western and Grant (Galveston) Avenues and on Preble Avenue in the borough of Manchester.

Two

ALLEGHENY CITY

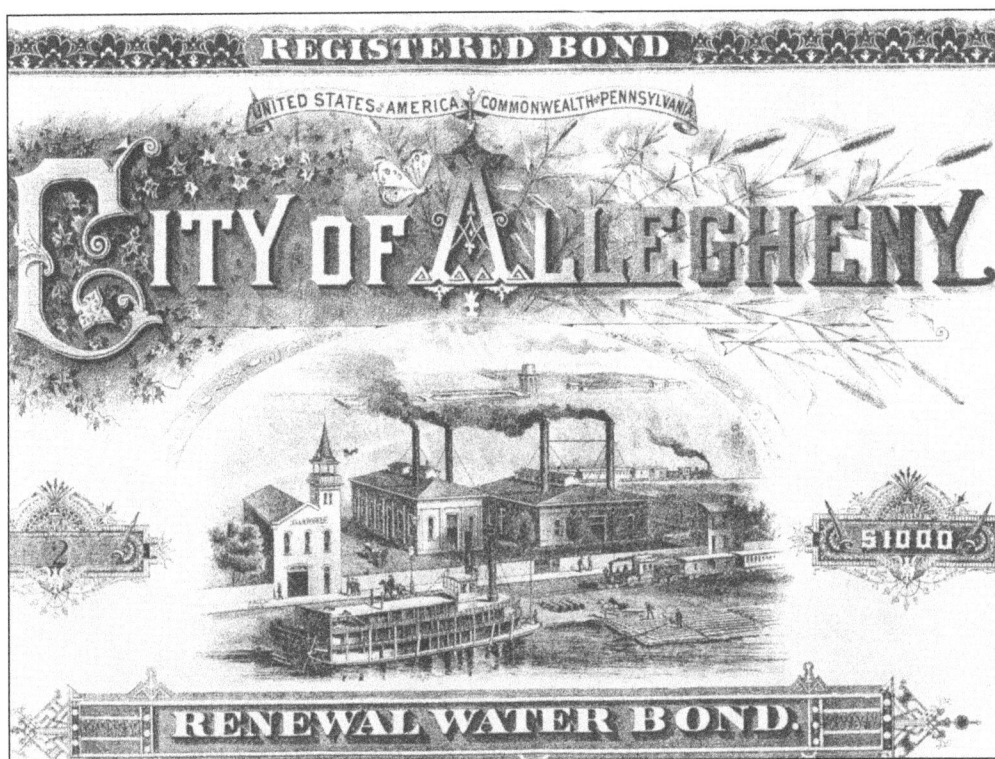

THE ALLEGHENY WATER BOND. The census of 1840 recorded that over 10,000 residents lived in the borough of Allegheny. In May of that year, Allegheny City was chartered by the government of Pennsylvania. The residential center began to shift to the "Second Bank" and beyond the common land. In 1847, the city government sought funding for the creation of a water system by selling bonds. This image on the Allegheny City water bond depicts an image of Allegheny's robust economy.

MAYOR FOSTER AND WIFE. William B. Foster, Allegheny City's third mayor (1842–1843), and his wife, Eliza Tomlinson Foster, are shown in this image. William held various posts in both state and national government prior to moving to Allegheny City. He also laid out the town of Lawrenceville prior to moving to Allegheny City. The Fosters had nine children, including the famous composer Stephen Collins Foster.

CASSATT FAMILY. Robert Cassatt, mayor of Allegheny City in 1846, resided with his family on Rebecca (Reedsdale) Street. Robert's wife, Catherine Johnston Cassatt, was educated at Anica Preble Barlow's school and attended, as a young girl, the reception for the Marquis de Lafayette at the Barlow home. Two of the Cassatt children pictured here became quite successful: Alexander as president of the Pennsylvania Railroad and Mary as the great impressionist painter.

MARKET HOUSE. During the years when Hezekiah Nixon served as mayor of Allegheny City, the first major market house was constructed at the southeast corner of Ohio and Federal Streets. The construction of a permanent market building provided a space for gardeners, dairymen, butchers, and tradesmen from the surrounding countryside to provide their wares to Allegheny's citizens on every day but Sunday.

FIRST FORT WAYNE RAILWAY STATION. Rail service came to Allegheny in 1851. Within a decade, rail lines were extended from Allegheny City along the Ohio River valley and on to Fort Wayne and Chicago. The lovely rail station pictured here is where Abraham Lincoln arrived on February 14, 1861, on the way to his inauguration. This was Lincoln's only visit in western Pennsylvania.

THE ALLEGHENY TRUST COMPANY AND THE DEUTSCHE NATIONAL BANK. The growth of commerce and manufacturing in Allegheny City in the years before the Civil War contributed to the need of banking establishments necessary for the accumulation of investment capital. The German-speaking population of Allegheny was quite significant, so banks were organized to serve both the German-speaking and the English-speaking communities. Pictured here are the Allegheny Trust Company, which was located on Federal Street, and the Deutsche National Bank, which was located on East Ohio Street.

Deutsche National Bank von Allegheny.

JOHN HEATH HOME. In the decade before the Civil War, John Heath was the owner of a planning mill on Fayette Street (North Avenue) in the borough of Manchester. Heath's home was located nearby his mill on Bageley Lane (Bidwell Street). At that time this area was considered in the countryside in that it was some distance from the center of Manchester and the center of Allegheny.

ARCHIBALD MARSHALL HOUSE. Archibald Marshall was a very successful businessman and banker. Marshall, a major grain and flour merchant in Allegheny, had one of the first grand homes built on Ridge Avenue. The house pictured here was constructed in 1851. Marshall, who had a great interest in botany, took an active part in the transformation of the common land across from his home into West Park.

JOHN BARR CLARK MARCH. At the outbreak of the Civil War, Rev. John Barr Clark was pastor at the Second United Presbyterian Church of Allegheny. An ardent abolitionist, Barr heeded Lincoln's call for troops, and he raised a company that became the 123rd Pennsylvania Regiment. The veterans of the 123rd were highly respected by their fellow Alleghenians. "Col. Clark's Grand Triumphant March" was composed to honor this local militant pastor.

ALEXANDER HAYS. Alexander Hays was the chief engineer of Allegheny City when the Civil War commenced. A graduate of Allegheny College and of West Point, Hays volunteered to return to military duty and recruited the 63rd Pennsylvania Regiment, which fought in many battles of the war. On May 5, 1864, Hays was mortally wounded in the Battle of the Wilderness. He was a highly regarded hero throughout Allegheny City.

CITY HALL, ALLEGHENY CITY.

NEW CITY HALL. In 1862, the political leaders of Allegheny City acted to have a new city hall constructed. They selected Charles Antoine Colomb Gengemere, a highly respected French architect who immigrated to America and resided in Allegheny, to design and oversee the construction of the building. The city hall was built for $60,000. When opened in 1864, it was considered by many architects to be a finely designed building.

MISS RACHEL MCFADDEN,
Secretary of Sanitary Commission.

RACHEL MCFADDEN. In June 1864, the civic leaders in Allegheny and Pittsburgh formed the Pittsburgh Sanitary Fair Commission as a means of raising funds to aid the troops fighting for the Union cause and their families. Rachel McFadden, a relative of Gen. Alexander Hays, took a leading role in the organization of this very successful event held in Allegheny City's new town hall and the public squares surrounding it.

29

SANITARY FAIR SCENE. Dr. Felix R. Brunot, a prominent citizen of Allegheny, chaired the Pittsburgh Sanitary Fair Commission. This is a photograph of the Women's Art Committee, which organized an exhibition of fine art works in the council chambers of Allegheny's new city hall. Several participating artists—George Hetzel, Trevor McClurg, and William C. White—are included in this scene.

SANITARY FAIR TABLEAUX. This artistic tableaux scene was one of the many features at the sanitary fair. The three women in the scene representing the healing arts are Lizzie Johnston, Kate McKnight, and Kate Brown. All three women were daughters of prominent civic and economic leaders of Allegheny City. The fair ran June 1–18, 1864, and raised $363,570 for the cause.

THE MONITOR BUILDING. Several temporary buildings were constructed in Allegheny's public square to house the exhibits at the sanitary fair. The Monitor Building, located next to the new Allegheny City Hall, was a main attraction. In this building was a man-made water exhibit in which a model of the *Monitor*, the Union's first ironclad vessel, was displayed.

JOHN ADAM GILLELAND. Prior to enlisting in Col. John Barr Clark's Union army regiment, John Adam Gilleland was a clerk who resided near Clark's church. He is pictured here in his uniform between two fellow soldiers from the 123rd Pennsylvania Regiment. In 1890, Pres. Benjamin Harrison appointed Gilleland to be the postmaster of Allegheny City.

AT LEWIS, OLIVER & PHILLIPS' LOWER MILL.

OLIVER IRON WORKS. The Civil War was a great catalyst for the economies of industrial centers throughout the Union. Allegheny City was no exception to this boom. The Lewis, Oliver, and Phillips Iron Works was established in lower Allegheny in 1866. The plant was located along the north bank of the Ohio River near the communities of Woods Run and Verner.

JOHN GILL, JR.'S, CAR WHEEL WORKS.

PITTSBURGH CAR WHEEL WORKS. This foundry was formed in 1870 by John L. Gill. It was the only foundry of its kind in the western Pennsylvania region, where the rail industry was growing at a rapid pace. Gill's foundry was located between Preble Avenue and the Ohio River in Manchester.

32

EBERHARDT AND OBER BREWERY. Political turmoil in the German states in the mid-19th century contributed to large numbers of German immigrants settling in the eastern wards of Allegheny. Both the Ober and Eberhardt families established small breweries in the years before the Civil War. Following that war, in 1870, John Ober and his brother-in-law William Eberhardt formed a successful partnership known as the Eberhardt and Ober Brewery.

OLD HONESTY SOAP. The meat-processing plants in the Spring Garden valley and on Herr's Island grew rapidly as the population of Allegheny and surrounding communities expanded in the years following the Civil War. The Old Honesty Soap works, using by-products from the slaughterhouses, was established in Spring Garden by the Falck family. Boxes of laundry soap were regularly delivered to many Allegheny homes.

CYCLORAMA. For several decades after the Civil War, there was high interest in its major battles, particularly the Battle of Gettysburg. A massive round building was constructed at the corner of Irwin Avenue (Brighton Road) and Beech Avenue to house a large painting of the pivotal events at Gettysburg. The cyclorama building also housed Luther's Ice Cream Parlor. It was a popular attraction in Allegheny in the late 19th century.

ALLEGHENY COUNTY CIVIL WAR MONUMENT. In 1869, Allegheny City offered a high site on Hogback Hill (later Seminary Hill and now Monument Hill) for the placement of a monument honoring those residents from the county who fought in the Civil War. There was some dispute over the site and another in Allegheny Cemetery. The Allegheny City site was chosen, and the monument was dedicated on Memorial Day 1871.

Three

ALLEGHENY CITY
EXPANDS

THE YOEDT FAMILY RESTAURANT. Population growth in Allegheny City and the surrounding communities in the Civil War years tended to blur the lines that separated one community from another. An economic interdependency also caused the leaders in Allegheny City and the adjoining boroughs to see advantages in political consolidation. Within a two-year period of 1867–1868, all of Manchester Borough, Duquesne Borough, sections of McClure and Reserve Townships, and parts of Troy Hill and Spring Garden were annexed to Allegheny City. The Yoedt family of Spring Garden probably saw definite advantages of being part of the flourishing Allegheny City.

THE YOEDT FAMILY. Yoedt's restaurant was located at 173–175 Spring Garden Avenue. John Yoedt emigrated from Hesse, and Rosina, his wife, was born in Wurtemburg. It was not surprising that they settled in a German-speaking neighborhood. There were eventually eight children in this family. This photograph was taken before the last four were born.

THE STERLINGS BASKETBALL TEAM. The Sterlings was the name of a basketball team comprised of boys from the Spring Garden neighborhood. In 1896, they were the champions in the Allegheny County Boys Junior Basketball League. The team was comprised of (first row) G. Billinger, W. Billinger, and ? Graham; (second row) ? Bertges, ? Sutton, ? McMahon, and ? Yoedt,

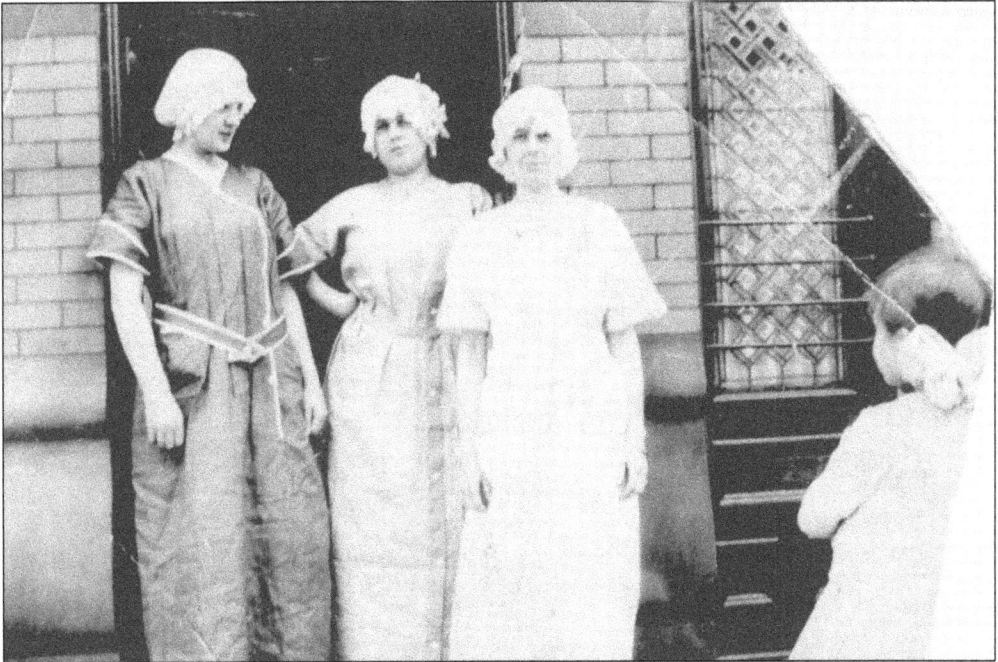

HOTEL RAHN. The Hotel Rahn was located at the corner of Second (Suismon) and Middle Streets. In the heart of Allegheny's Dutchtown, Rahn's was both a tavern and hotel with a definite German flavor. This photograph is of three of the young women employees taking a break from their day's work in the hotel.

RAHN FAMILY. This group portrait is of the family of George and Katherine Neagely Rahn and 10 of their 11 children. The Rahn family lived in the large building that contained both the tavern and the Hotel Rahn.

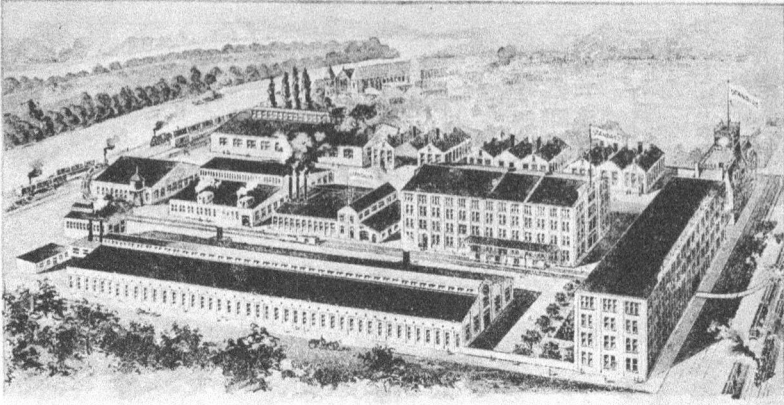

STANDARD MANUFACTURING COMPANY,

THE largest plant in the world devoted exclusively to the manufacture of PORCELAIN ENAMELED BATHS and PLUMBING GOODS.

FACTORY,
551-583 PREBLE AVENUE, ALLEGHENY.

STANDARD MANUFACTURING COMPANY. Mid-19th-century American cities saw the construction of water and sewer systems allowing for homes to include indoor plumbing. In 1875, two enterprising businessmen of Allegheny City, James W. Arrott and Francis Torrence, founded the Standard Manufacturing Company. Located along the Ohio River in Allegheny's Ninth Ward, the company's plumbing products were sold throughout America.

FRANCIS J. TORRENCE. This founder of the Standard Manufacturing Company was married to the daughter of Rev. Adoniram Bonsall, pastor of the Sandusky Street Baptist Church. Influenced by the "social gospel" preaching of Bonsall, Francis J. Torrence acted to improve the quality of life in the community near the company's plant. He took a leading role in establishing the Woods Run Settlement House.

TURNVEREIN. Immigrants coming to America brought with them many of the customs and institutions of their homeland. Many 19th-century immigrants from the German states established Turnverein organizations and built Turner halls. The Allegheny Turn Halle was built on South Canal Street. Turnverein programs included gymnastics, political discussion groups, and social festivities.

PITTSBURGH AND ALLEGHENY TRACTION CREW. The replacement of horse-drawn trolleys with those powered by electricity impacted residential developments in cities throughout America. The work crew building the first electric trolley system in Allegheny City, seen in this photograph, set the stage for the development of housing in the very outskirts of the city and the "streetcar suburbs" beyond.

THOMPSON HOME ON LINCOLN AVENUE. In the 1880s and 1890s, many of Allegheny City's wealthiest families built homes on streets to the west of the commons, which had been transformed into a beautifully designed urban park. William Reed Thompson, a highly successful banker, and his wife, Mary Thaw Thompson, established their family home at 39 Lincoln Avenue, a few doors from Mary's brother William Thaw Jr.

THOMPSON FAMILY PORTRAIT. William and Mary Thaw Thompson, with their children, sit for a family portrait in one of the parlors of their home. The furnishing and decor of the parlor provide a glimpse of the lifestyle of one of the elite Allegheny families.

THOMPSON FAMILY HOME PARLOR. One biographer of William R. Thompson remarked that "he joined no clubs, but sought in his library and home the enjoyment of his leisure hours." Evidence of this can be seen in this view of the double parlor in the Thompson home.

THOMPSON FAMILY HOME. The Thompsons had a family of five children. Mary's room on the second floor of the home gives clear evidence of her role as a mother, a voracious reader, and a woman who made great use of her writing desk.

NEWCOMER HEARSE. With the coming of the electric trolley Alleghenians were able to ride up and beyond the crest of Perrysville Avenue. This community beyond the crest became a desirable residential area. In that hilltop neighborhood, William and Ada Newcomer established a funeral home at 2108 Perrysville Avenue to serve the families moving there. This horse-drawn hearse was used by the Newcomer Funeral Home.

ADA NEWCOMER. William Newcomer died at a fairly young age. Paul's widow, Ada, took over the management and operation of the Newcomer Funeral Home. Ada Newcomer was the first woman in the county to own and operate a funeral home. She continued in this capacity for several decades following her husband's death.

BASKET VENDOR AT THE ALLEGHENY MARKET. In the last quarter of the 19th century, economic activity in and around the Allegheny Market House was very dynamic. All trolley lines passed through the intersection at Federal and Ohio Streets. The constant flow of customers was welcomed by craftsmen such as this basket vendor whose stand was at one of the entrances to the market house.

HOMER TURK. Surrounding the four large public squares at the very center of Allegheny City was a ring of streets. They all were called Diamond Street but designated by which side of the square they were located: North Diamond, West Diamond, and so on. Many small shops were located on these side streets. One such shop, on East Diamond, was that of Homer Turk, purveyor of fresh produce and melons.

Deutsche Apotheke.

PURE DRUGS, PAINTS,

OILS, VARNISHES &C.

FRED. H. EGGERS,
Druggist and Apothecary,
172 Ohio Street, Corner Middle, Allegheny, Pa.
Physicians' Prescriptions Carefully Compounded at all Hours.

EGGERS GERMAN DRUGSTORE. When walking east along Ohio Street from the Allegheny City center, more and more of the stores and shops would be transacting business and socializing on the sidewalk in the German language. A good example of a drugstore in Dutchtown was Fred Eggers Deutsche Apotheke.

GIRL WITH RADISH BOUQUET. In the 1870s and 1880s, many immigrants from central and eastern Europe settled in the Woods Run neighborhood where work could be found in the rail yards and factories located along the rail lines and the Ohio River. This young girl, perhaps from a Ukrainian, Russian, or Slovak family, holds a bouquet of radishes from her family's garden.

CZECHO-SLOVAK BAND. Music, often a powerful force binding communities together, was evident in Allegheny's Welsh choirs in Woods Run and the German *mannerchors* and *liedertafels* scattered throughout the German neighborhoods. The Czecho-Slovak band pictured here probably performed at the Bohemian National Hall located on Vinial Street in Allegheny's Seventh Ward.

RIVERSIDE PENITENTIARY OF WESTERN PENNSYLVANIA. This prison was built in 1886 along the bank of the Ohio River in the Woods Run neighborhood. When it was completed, the 1827 prison in the commons was leveled. A music pavilion was built at that site.

THE HIGH BRIDGE. Constructed in the mid-1890s, this bridge crossed the Jack's Run valley that separated Allegheny City from Bellevue. The trolley line from Allegheny City was extended to Bellevue over the High Bridge. Beneath the bridge was farmland owned by the Zaph family, including a pond filled from Jack's Run. Known as Zaph's Pond, it was used for ice-skating for youngsters living in the Davisville section of Allegheny's Eleventh Ward.

ALLEGHENY COUNTRY CLUB. After bridges were built over the Woods Run and the Jack's Run valleys, a trolley line was built along the California Avenue corridor connecting the center of Allegheny City with its outer edges. In Davisville, the city's westernmost neighborhood, the Allegheny Country Club was organized to provide a golf course (only nine holes) for many of the wealthy families of Allegheny.

COAL BARGES AND GAS TANK. Two major reasons for the success of the iron and steel industries of the region were the proximity to river transportation and the great coal seam that stretched throughout western Pennsylvania. Both of these factors are evident in this view of Allegheny City's shoreline along the Allegheny and Ohio Rivers. In the background is the massive storage tank of the Allegheny Gas Company. Considered to be the largest tank of its type in the world, the tank was constructed along Rebecca (Reedsdale) Street. It stored the natural gas necessary to provide that resource needed to illuminate and heat the growing number of homes, businesses, and institutions in the city. The number of coal barges and the size of the gas tank are vivid symbols of the strength of Allegheny City's economic condition at the dawn of the 20th century.

STEURNAGEL HARDWARE STORE. A boom in the housing market certainly accompanied the growth surge of Allegheny's population in the 1890s. This led to an increasing market for all the necessary tools and supplies of the building trades. Hardware stores, such as this one owned and operated by the Steurnagel family in the busy commercial core of East Ohio Street, were well stocked with the thousands of items needed by home builders and residents alike.

HAVEKOTTE JEWELRY SHOP. The posh interior of the Havekotte Jewelry Shop, located on East Ohio Street in the heart of Dutchtown, provides some indication of the strength of the economy in Allegheny City at the dawn of the 20th century. The Havekotte family, which had settled in Reserve Township in the mid-19th century, was quite prominent in a number of business and banks that catered to the German-speaking community.

Four

CONGREGATIONS

ST. PETER'S CATHEDRAL. The earliest residents of Allegheny Town arrived mostly from the eastern parts of Pennsylvania or from the British Isles and German principalities. These settlers adhered to various Protestant belief systems, and the earliest congregations formed in the first few decades of the 19th century reflected these traditions. In the 1830s, the population of Allegheny grew rapidly, and the ethnic and religious communities became more diverse. Among the immigrants from Ireland and Germany were many Roman Catholics, and among the German immigrants were a significant number of Jews. In 1876, St. Peter's, an Irish parish, was designated the cathedral of the newly formed, and short-lived, Diocese of Allegheny.

Pro-Cathedral, Allegheny.

BISHOP MICHAEL DOMENEC. In 1876, the Spanish-born priest Michael Domenec was bishop of Pittsburgh. He encouraged the Vatican to divide the Diocese of Pittsburgh in two. All the territory north of the Allegheny River was named the Diocese of Allegheny, with Domenec as bishop of Allegheny. Domenec died the following year in Spain, and the Diocese of Allegheny was returned to the authority of the bishop of Pittsburgh.

ST. MARY'S CATHOLIC CHURCH. Until 1848, the German-speaking Catholics of Allegheny had to travel to St. Philomena's Church in Pittsburgh to hear mass in German. In 1848, the bishop of Pittsburgh authorized the establishment of a parish in Allegheny for the German Catholic community living there. St. Mary's became the mother church for other German Catholic parishes in Manchester, Troy Hill, and the East Street valley.

ST. ANTHONY'S CHAPEL. When the Most Holy Name of Jesus parish was opened in 1868 for the German Catholic community on Troy Hill, Bishop Michael Domenec assigned Fr. Suitbert G. Mollinger as parish priest. Mollinger came from a family of considerable wealth. From these private resources he paid for the building of the St. Anthony's Chapel in 1880. Here he placed his extensive collection of holy relics.

ST. ANTHONY'S CHAPEL, TROY HILL, ALLEGHENY.

ST. NICHOLAS CATHOLIC CHURCH. Employment opportunities in industries along the Allegheny River in the last quarter of the 19th century drew many families from Croatia to Allegheny City's Eighth Ward. In 1894, Fr. Dobroslav Josip Bozic met with Bishop Phelan to plan for the formation of the St. Nicholas congregation, the first Croatian Catholic parish in America. This church building was dedicated in January 1895.

ST. JOHN'S LUTHERAN CHURCH. The first Lutheran church in Allegheny, St. John's, was gathered by Pastor J. C. F. Heyer in 1837. The congregation, located in Dutchtown, conducted all business and all services in the German language. It was the mother church of several Lutheran congregations in Allegheny as well as the founder of St. John's Hospital, St. John's Orphanage, and St. John's Home for the Aged.

TRINITY LUTHERAN CHURCH. Until 1860, those Lutherans in Allegheny City who preferred the use of the English language had to travel to the First English Lutheran Church in Pittsburgh. In 1846, Pastor W. A. Passavant of that congregation opened a mission in Allegheny. In 1860, the First English Lutheran Church of Allegheny (later called Trinity Lutheran Church) was organized. In 1872, the congregation dedicated this church building on Stockton Avenue.

MOUNT ZION LUTHERAN CHURCH. As the population began to move out from the original town center, new religious communities were founded. The congregation of Mount Zion Lutheran Church was gathered from among the residents in the Tenth Ward of Allegheny. With support from Passavant and other Lutheran congregations in Allegheny, a plot of land was purchased on Franklin Road. In 1879, this frame building was dedicated.

CONFIRMATION CLASS, ST. PETER'S EVANGELICAL LUTHERAN. This image is of the confirmation class of the St. Peter's Evangelical Lutheran Church. The church was located in the Fourth Ward of Allegheny. It is evident by the announcement signs on both sides of the church entrance that both English and German services were conducted here.

EMMANUEL EPISCOPAL CHURCH. In the mid-19th century, the Emmanuel Episcopal congregation was formed in Manchester. In 1885–1886, the congregation contracted with the renowned architect H. H. Richardson to design this church building, located at the intersection of Allegheny and North Avenues. The church building was tagged as "the bake-oven church" because of Richardson's curved design at the back of the building.

ST. AUGUSTINE MISSION. The St. Augustine mission was located on Jackson (Jacksonia) Street in 1904. This mission was headed by Rev. Scott Wood as a means of the Episcopal denomination reaching out to the African American community in Allegheny City.

CALVARY METHODIST CHURCH
(EXTERIOR). When fire destroyed
the Christ Methodist Church
in the central business district
of Pittsburgh, the leaders of the
congregation decided to build
two new church buildings. Those
members of the congregation
residing in Allegheny City opted
for this stone neo-Gothic-style
building that was constructed
at the corner of Allegheny and
Beech Avenues in 1892–1893.

CALVARY METHODIST CHURCH (INTERIOR). Architectural historian James D. Van Trump
referred to the interior of the Calvary Methodist Church as "the ecclesiastical counterpart to
a proper Victorian parlor." The interior of the church was given a feeling of grandeur from the
light pouring through three magnificent windows produced at the Tiffany studios. The Horne,
Shea, Verner, and Scaife families generously supported this congregation.

GERMAN BAPTIST CHURCH. In the German-speaking communities of Allegheny, along with the traditional German denominations, there were also German Baptists, German Methodists, and German Presbyterian congregations. The original German Baptist church was located at the corner of East and First (Foreland) Streets. When many of its congregants moved farther out the East Street valley, this new church was built at East and Creek Streets.

First German
Presbyterian
Church

REV J LAUNITZ,
PASTOR

GERMAN PRESBYTERIAN CHURCH. The First (and only) German Presbyterian Church of Allegheny was gathered by Rev. John Launitz in 1859. The church building was built in the 1860s on Sampson (Juniata) Street in Manchester. Launitz was the only pastor of the congregation. He ministered to this community from 1859 to 1913. The baptismal records reveal that Launitz was fluent in German, English, French, and Italian.

FIRST CHRISTIAN CHURCH OF ALLEGHENY. One of the largest congregations throughout the history of Allegheny City was that of the First Christian (Disciples) Church of Allegheny Town. This denomination had its roots in western Pennsylvania through the teachings of Thomas and Alexander Campbell. The church building in this image was located at the corner of Montgomery and Arch Streets.

FIRST CHRISTIAN CHURCH, ALLEGHENY, PA.

SANDUSKY STREET BAPTIST CHURCH. Baptist traditions with their roots in European Anabaptist movements were brought to Allegheny Town with settlers from England and Wales. The first Baptist chapel (1835) was located on Robinson Street opposite the Arbuckles and Avery cotton factory. The congregation's second church building, shown here, was built on Sandusky Street in 1843.

57

METROPOLITAN BAPTIST CHURCH. As the congregation of the Sandusky Street Baptist Church grew in size, a group of African Americans left to establish its own congregation in 1847. The Metropolitan Baptist Church, located on Sampson (Sampsonia) Street, was founded in Allegheny in 1860. This congregation constructed the church building shown here in 1905.

BROWN CHAPEL. Deed records show that in the years before the Civil War the property at Boyle and Hemlock Streets in Allegheny City's Third Ward was purchased for use by an African American congregation. This congregation, the Brown Chapel African Methodist Episcopal, originated in 1837–1838 as one of the oldest African Methodist Episcopal congregations in western Pennsylvania.

FOURTH UNITED PRESBYTERIAN CHURCH. The Fourth United Presbyterian Church of Allegheny was organized in 1860 with support from the denominational leaders in the community. In 1866, the congregation was able to construct the church building seen here. Included in this congregation were two women who were strong advocates for improving the quality of life for many children: Dr. Jane Vincent and Mary Junkin Cowley.

Rev. James M. Fulton, D.D.
"The Man of Vision"

REV. JAMES M. FULTON. In 1877, when he was a senior at the Western Theological Seminary, Rev. James M. Fulton was called to the pastorate of the Fourth United Presbyterian Church of Allegheny. He served in that capacity until 1890. It was under his leadership and vision that the United Presbyterian Orphans' Home and Memorial Hospital were established in Allegheny City.

NORTH PRESBYTERIAN CHURCH. At the outset of the Civil War, a dispute arose within the congregation of the Central Presbyterian Church of Allegheny over the pastor's refusal to speak supportively of the North. In April 1863, unhappy congregants left the church and organized a new congregation called North Presbyterian Church. In 1870, the congregation constructed the building shown here at the corner of Lincoln and Grant (Galveston) Avenues.

BOHEMIAN PRESBYTERIAN CHURCH PICNIC. Many of the residents living in the western section of Troy Hill were emigrants from the Czech regions of the Austro-Hungarian Empire. While most of these families attended St. Wenceslaus, the Czech Catholic parish, a smaller number of families organized the Bohemian Presbyterian Church. The image here is of a church picnic in Riverview Park of this congregation.

CONCORDIA CLUB. Among the many German immigrants coming to Allegheny City in the 19th century were Jewish families. Rodef Shalom, the largest and oldest congregation of Jews, was in Pittsburgh. The Concordia Club, a town club to which many a successful Jew belonged, was in Allegheny. In November 1885, a conference of rabbis met at the Concordia Club and framed "the Pittsburgh Platform," a belief statement of Reform Judaism.

BETH ISRAEL. Beth Israel was a congregation comprised of Jewish families who lived and worked in the eastern neighborhoods in Allegheny City. Many of these families had emigrated from Poland, Austria-Hungary, and Russia. In 1905, they purchased the original church building on East Street from the German Baptist congregation and transformed the interior of the building into their own synagogue.

CHARLES TAZE RUSSELL. The founder of the Jehovah's Witness movement was born in Allegheny City in 1852. Following a short and rather successful career as a businessman, Charles Taze Russell turned to issues of religion. In 1879, he began the publication of religious tracts that explained his religious beliefs. Within a few years, the Watch Tower Tract Society was formed and incorporated. This became the basis of the Jehovah's Witness denomination.

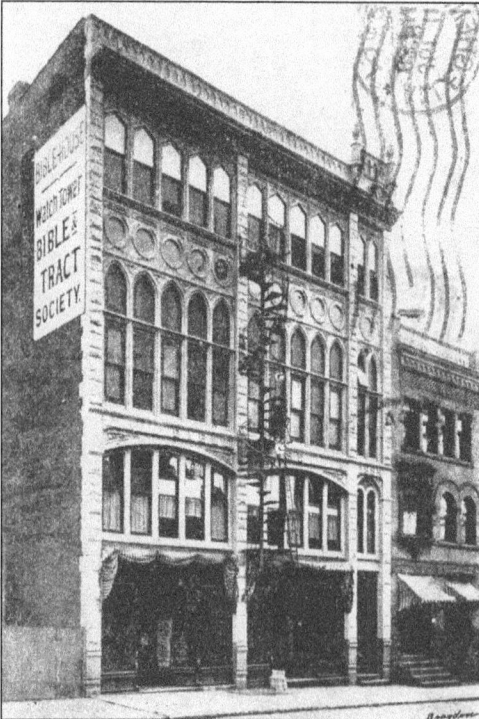

BIBLE HOUSE. Charles Taze Russell established the Bible House as the publication center of the Watch Tower Tract Society. It was originally located on Federal Street in Allegheny City, and as the movement grew, the publishing work done at the Bible House was transferred to a larger facility, Bethel House, in Brooklyn, New York.

Five

CARING INSTITUTIONS

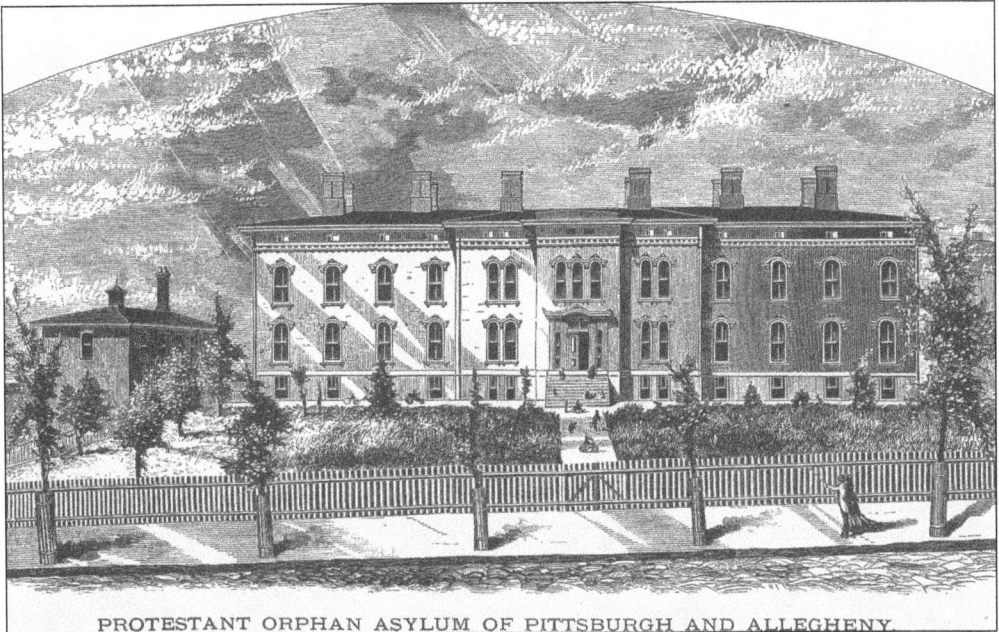

PROTESTANT ORPHAN ASYLUM OF PITTSBURGH AND ALLEGHENY.

PROTESTANT ORPHAN ASYLUM. In American cities throughout the 19th century, the issues of sickness, disease, agedness, destitution, and death were visible in every neighborhood. Allegheny City was no exception. The most vulnerable were the young and the old. The issue of caring for those who had no one to advocate their cause was frequently brought to the fore by religious institutions. In 1832, a group of women from Allegheny and Pittsburgh formed the Orphan Asylum of Pittsburgh and Allegheny and opened a building to house the children in 1838. In 1860, a larger and better-appointed orphans' home was constructed at the corner of Ridge and Grant (Galveston) Avenues.

DR. C. JANE VINCENT. The daughter of the founder of Westminster College in New Wilmington, Charity Jane Vincent, M.D., graduated from the Women's Medical College in Philadelphia. In 1882, she began the practice of medicine in Allegheny City. Vincent took a leading role in the founding of the United Presbyterian Orphans' Home and of the Memorial Hospital, both located at Jefferson and Monterey Streets.

UNITED PRESBYTERIAN MEMORIAL HOSPITAL. Ten years after the establishment of the United Presbyterian orphanage, it was evident that medical care was a growing need, not only among the children in the orphanage but within the broader community. In 1889, a small hospital was established near the orphanage. Vincent was president of the hospital board. By 1906, the hospital had been relocated in Wilkinsburg and renamed Columbia Hospital.

UNITED PRESBYTERIAN ORPHANAGE. Rev. James M. Fulton, a young and visionary pastor of the Fourth United Presbyterian Church of Allegheny, gathered together a group of women from congregations in Pittsburgh and Allegheny to address the need of orphaned children. In 1880, two years after this meeting, the United Presbyterian orphanage was opened at the corner of Jefferson and Monterey Streets in Allegheny's Second Ward.

UNITED PRESBYTERIAN ORPHANAGE NURSERY. The governing board of the United Presbyterian orphanage was comprised of women drawn from a number of congregations. These women strongly believed that the life of youngsters in the orphanage should mirror life in a typical middle-class home. A nursery room was provided with the types of toys and games that might easily have been found in the home of any of the board members.

UNITED PRESBYTERIAN ORPHANAGE CLASSROOM. As an institution governed by a group of churchwomen, space would have been created for some form of religious education and worship. In this classroom of the United Presbyterian orphanage, the youngsters can be seen in their Sunday best. The portrait on the wall above the mantle is that of Rev. James M. Fulton, who had been the great advocate for the children.

THE HOME FOR THE FRIENDLESS. Desertion, destitution, and death were forces contributing the large numbers of orphaned children or youngsters with parents unable to care for them. The Home for the Friendless was established in 1861. In 1887, a massive stone double house on Washington (Pressley) Street became the permanent location of the Home for the Friendless.

ST. JOSEPH'S ORPHANAGE. It is not surprising that a home for the orphans of German Catholic families would be located on Troy Hill. Here was a community that seemed to be a transplant of a German village on American soil. The St. Joseph's Orphanage was supported by all the German-speaking parishes in the Pittsburgh diocese and operated by the Sisters de Notre Dame.

ST. PETER'S ORPHANAGE. The St. Peter's Evangelical Lutheran congregation on Lockhart Street seems to have been greatly influenced by the social gospel message that spread throughout many urban Protestant congregations in the late 19th century. In the 1890s, the congregation established and supported an orphanage on Robinson (Rockledge) Street on Spring Hill.

JACOB GUSKY. Jacob Gusky owned one of the largest and most successful department stores in Pittsburgh. A leader within the Jewish community and a prominent member of the Rodef Shalom congregation, Gusky was very benevolent to institutions that cared for children in both Pittsburgh and Allegheny. He frequently sent gifts during the Christmas season to many of the Christian orphanages.

THE GUSKY ORPHANAGE. As a memory to her husband, following his untimely death, Esther Gusky funded the establishment of an orphanage for Jewish children. The Gusky Orphanage received additional support from many families in the Jewish community. The orphanage was located in the Tenth Ward of Allegheny at the intersection of Riverview and Perrysville Avenues.

68

HOME OF THE GOOD SHEPHERD. A group of Sisters of the Good Shepherd came to Allegheny City from Buffalo, New York, to establish a convent and develop a mission to work with young girls who were orphaned or in trouble with the law. A cloister, where the sisters lived, and a separate home, for the girls under their care, were built at a site on Lowrie Street in the Troy Hill community.

THE CIVIL WAR WIDOWS HOME. The focus of the Allegheny Widows' Home Association, incorporated in 1860, was to provide decent housing for "poor widows and elderly maidens." During the Civil War years, the association advocated for the widows of fallen soldiers. The original building of the Protestant Orphan Asylum was purchased and opened to widows in 1866. In 1904, the association expanded to this home on Arlington (Armandale) Street.

ALLEGHENY GENERAL HOSPITAL, 1886. In 1881, a group of prominent leaders of Allegheny City met at the home of Mayor Lewis Peterson Jr. The result of this meeting was a plan to establish a nonsectarian general hospital in Allegheny. In 1882, the charter of the Allegheny Hospital was approved by the state, and by three years later, two homes on Stockton Avenue had been purchased and converted to a 30-room hospital.

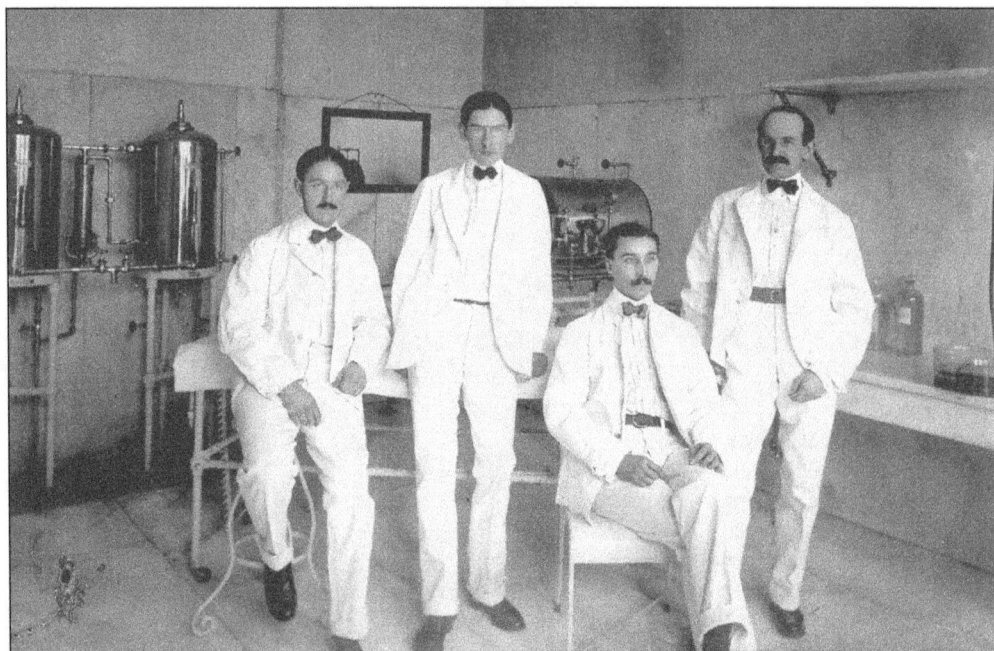

ALLEGHENY GENERAL HOSPITAL OPERATING ROOM. After opening in 1886, the Allegheny General Hospital medical staff continued to grow in number and to improve methods of treatment and care. By 1889, nearby property on Sandusky Street was acquired, thus providing more patient rooms. This image of the operating room at the hospital provides insight into the working environment of surgeons in the early 20th century.

ALLEGHENY GENERAL HOSPITAL NURSES. A pediatric department was opened at Allegheny General Hospital in 1887. That same year, plans were developed for the establishment of a school of nursing. The annual report of the hospital in 1892 stated that there were 35 students enrolled in the nursing school's three-year program. The graduating nurses shown in this image are posed at the Stockton Avenue entrance to the hospital.

Allegheny General Hospital & Park, Allegheny, Pa

ALLEGHENY GENERAL HOSPITAL, 1904. As the population of Allegheny City grew in the final decades of the 19th century, so too did the need for hospital services and care. Realizing the limitations of space in the 1886 building, the hospital's board of directors began to plan for a new hospital facility. In 1904, the new Allegheny General Hospital opened with room for 400 patients, a laboratory, and a pharmacy.

LOUISE LYLE, M.D. Louise Lyle, the founder of the Presbyterian Hospital of Pittsburgh, graduated at the age of 50 from the Presbyterian Women's Medical College in Cincinnati. She arrived in Allegheny City in 1893 and established the Louise Lyle Hospital at 31 North Sherman Avenue. This former residence had only five rooms for the treatment of patients. The hospital's first patient was brought to Lyle by Dr. Jane Vincent.

Dr. Louise J. Lyle, 1842–1932, Founder of Presbyterian Hospital

PRESBYTERIAN HOSPITAL, 1893–1900. In 1894, Lyle and the board of managers of the Lyle Hospital changed the name of the hospital to the Presbyterian Hospital of Pittsburgh. The following year, the hospital was legally incorporated. A need for additional space resulted in the purchase of the adjacent residence at 30 North Sherman Avenue. Within a span of two years the hospital had almost doubled its space.

72

PRESBYTERIAN HOSPITAL, 1900. By the last years of the 19th century, the growing demand for hospital treatment in Allegheny City and Pittsburgh pushed the directors of the Presbyterian Hospital to move to a more spacious facility. In 1900, the hospital acquired Dr. Sutton's Hospital, a handsomely designed privately owned hospital located on Ridge Avenue. The Presbyterian Hospital remained on Ridge Avenue until 1914.

ST. JOHN'S HOSPITAL. The leaders of the St. John's Lutheran congregation on Madison Avenue in Allegheny's Dutchtown took the lead in the establishment of St. John's Hospital in the distant Eleventh Ward. The need was great for a hospital near the industrial plants in Manchester, Woods Run, and Verner. F. J. Osterling designed the building, and when it opened in 1896, it was staffed by Lutheran deaconesses.

73

LITTLE SISTERS OF THE POOR. Early in the 1870s, the order of the Little Sisters of the Poor established a residential facility on Washington (Pressley) Street in Allegheny's Fourth Ward. Here the sisters cared for the aged poor residents of the city. The sisters and some of their residents would go throughout the neighborhoods in their "begging buggy" seeking food, clothing, and money for the poor and elderly folks under their care.

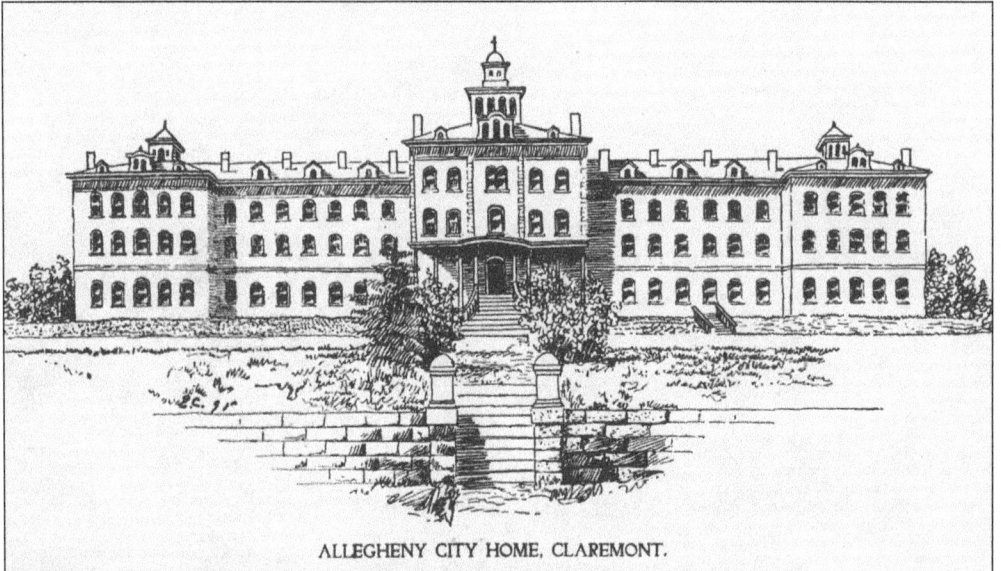

ALLEGHENY CITY HOME, CLAREMONT.

CLAREMONT. In 1844, the political leaders of Allegheny City appointed a commission to establish a publicly funded home for the "poor and indigent" of the city. The following year, the Allegheny City Home was opened on a site in Shaler Township. That site, in the village of Millvale, was sold in the late 1860s. A new city home, Claremont, on a tract of land facing the Allegheny River in O'Hara Township was opened in June 1873.

74

Six

SCHOOLING IN ALLEGHENY

FOURTH WARD SCHOOL. Alexis de Tocqueville, when traveling through many communities on the American frontier, wrote in a very positive manner of the commitment in these communities to universal education. In the earliest years of Allegheny Town, schools were established for the children in the various neighborhoods. The first schoolhouses were often connected with the religious congregations. Small private academies for boys and girls were organized as well. It was not long before one or more publicly funded school buildings were built in each of the Allegheny City's wards. The Fourth Ward School on Cedar Avenue is pictured here.

FIRST WARD SCHOOL. Allegheny City's First Ward was located along the Allegheny River on the west side of Federal Street. It was one of the earliest settled neighborhoods. In 1844, the first school building was constructed there on Rebecca (Reedsdale) Street. The renowned Prof. John Kelly was both principal and teacher here. Among his pupils were the Carnegie, Phipps, and Oliver boys.

SEVENTH WARD SCHOOL. After sections of Reserve Township were annexed to Allegheny, the community became the Seventh Ward. To most residents living there, the neighborhood was simply Spring Garden. The Spring Garden school building behind the youngsters in this class picture was built in 1888. It contained 12 rooms, which was a fairly large elementary school for that time.

MARY J. COWLEY SCHOOL CLASS PICTURE, 1902. The Mary J. Cowley School was originally one of three schools located in Allegheny City's Second Ward. It was named to honor Mary Junkin Cowley, a tireless advocate for Allegheny's children. James Dorsey, standing at the far left in the top row, went on to study at the University of Pittsburgh. Dorsey became the highly regarded leader of the Washington Recreation Center in Pittsburgh's Hill District.

ST. JOHN'S LUTHERAN SCHOOL. Within the German-speaking communities in the eastern wards of Allegheny City, many families desired that their youngsters be educated in the German language. The St. John's congregation on Madison Avenue established a parish school for children in that community. Later generations in this parish began sending their students to the public schools, and this school was closed.

St. Joseph's School. The St. Joseph's Roman Catholic parish was created in 1866 to serve the German Catholic community in Manchester Borough. One of the first acts of the parish leaders was the construction of a parish school. This classical-style schoolhouse was adjacent to the church. Originally the teaching staff was laymen, but in 1876, Benedictine nuns from Carrolltown took charge of the school.

Most Holy Name of Jesus School. Both St. Joseph's parish in Manchester and the Most Holy Name of Jesus parish in Troy Hill were established in 1866. The first pastor in Troy Hill, Fr. Suitbert G. Mollinger, immediately upon arriving at his new post, encouraged the parish leaders to establish a school in a section of his residence. In 1874, a new school building, shown here, was constructed to meet the needs of this growing congregation.

ALLEGHENY HIGH SCHOOL. The first citywide high school in Allegheny was organized in 1883 at a site on Sherman Avenue, formerly used as a school for the African American community. Additional property adjacent to the school building was acquired. Frederick J. Osterling won a competition for designing the new high school, and in 1889, the Osterling-designed building was opened.

ALLEGHENY HIGH SCHOOL CLASS PICTURE. The 1890 graduating class from Allegheny High School is seen in this image. Allegheny High School at this time was the only public high school in Allegheny County north of the Allegheny and Ohio Rivers. Some of the students in the class traveled a considerable distance to attend this school.

WILLA CATHER. During the years 1903–1906, one of the English teachers at Allegheny High School was Willa Cather. Cather had come to the area to work for a local women's magazine. When she left that position she was hired to teach in Pittsburgh and a few years later at Allegheny High School. Harriet Kelly, a student in Cather's class, remarked about how inspiring Cather was as a teacher.

PARK INSTITUTE. One of the effects of an industrializing community was the need for skilled personnel for positions in the offices of the growing number of companies. The Park Institute was established to provide men and women the skills necessary to move into this job market. The institute had two locations facing the commons, one on West North Avenue near Federal Street and the other on Cedar Avenue.

FIRST ALLEGHENY OBSERVATORY BUILDING. A group of scientists and learned businessmen organized the Allegheny Telescope Association in 1859. Reorganized in 1860 as the Allegheny Observatory Society, the group built an observatory building at a highly elevated site on Perrysville Avenue where they installed their new 13-inch telescope. In 1867, the observatory became part of the astronomy department of the Western University of Pennsylvania.

ALLEGHENY OBSERVATORY.

THE ALLEGHENY OBSERVATORY.

ALLEGHENY OBSERVATORY, C. 1875. When the Allegheny Observatory was consolidated with the astronomy department of the Western University of Pennsylvania, it became desirable to expand the building for classrooms, offices, and laboratories. This newly expanded observatory complex would be easily fitted into the campus of the university that was to move to the Perrysville Avenue site by 1890.

WESTERN UNIVERSITY OF PENNSYLVANIA. Founded in the late 18th century as the Pittsburgh Academy, the Western University of Pennsylvania was located in the center of Pittsburgh until 1882. After relocating to several buildings on North Avenue in Allegheny City for a few years, a new site for the university's core program was selected. It was adjacent to the already established Allegheny Observatory on what had become known as Observatory Hill.

STEIN SISTERS. The first two women to receive degrees from the Western University of Pennsylvania graduated in 1898. They were two sisters: Stella Mathilda Stein and Margaret Lydia Stein. The sisters had identical grades, which were the highest in the graduating class. They both received degrees in "Latin Scientific."

CHANCELLOR'S OFFICE. In 1892, the Western University of Pennsylvania became the University of Pittsburgh. Departments of the university were located in several sections of Pittsburgh and Allegheny. The administrative center and most classrooms were at the Perrysville Avenue campus. It was from this chancellor's office that the university was managed.

WESTERN THEOLOGICAL SEMINARY. Founded in 1827, the Western Theological Seminary developed over the following decades to a major training school for Presbyterian pastors. In the late 19th century, it was one of three different seminaries bordering the commons that were identified with some branch of Presbyterian tradition. This building, facing Ridge Avenue, was used for classes, offices, and some student residences.

ALLEGHENY SEMINARY. With its founding by Rev. John Taylor Pressly at the First Associate Reformed Presbyterian Church of Allegheny Town, the Allegheny Seminary continued in the preparation of pastors. In 1858, the name of the denomination overseeing this seminary became the United Presbyterian Church in North America. In 1899, the Allegheny Seminary opened its new building on North Avenue at Buena Vista Street.

REFORMED PRESBYTERIAN SEMINARY. Reformed Presbyterians were often called Covenanters, referring to events in Scotland during the 17th century. Given the number of Scots who settled in western Pennsylvania, it was not surprising to find a number of Reformed Presbyterian congregations. It was for that reason that, in 1838, Allegheny Town was selected as the site for a seminary. In 1872, the seminary was located in this building on North Avenue.

Seven

PARKS AND MONUMENTS

JUBILEE DAY. "Today is Jubilee Day! No school today! This is the day we go to the park!" The tradition in many of the schools in Allegheny City was to end the school year by spending the day in the park. Here the students from Manchester School are marching, class by class, on their way to a day in Allegheny City's park. In 1869, city leaders moved to convert the common land into parkland. By the 1890s, the Allegheny Park was one of the most beautiful urban parks in the nation. In the same decade, the city acted to create a larger, more naturalistic park, Riverview Park, in the Tenth Ward. To the citizens of Allegheny, the parks were a treasure.

THE NORTH COMMONS, 1864. From the early years of the settlement of Allegheny, the 100 acres of common land around the town center had been used for grazing. With the passage of time, it had become more of an unattended dumping ground. This image of a lone cow, along with the housing along North Avenue, gives a view of the conditions on and around the common land shortly before it became parkland.

LAKE ELIZABETH. The idyllic view across Lake Elizabeth is reminiscent of an Old World village green. In the plan for the development of the park, the landscape-designing firm of Grant and Mitchell called for the creation of a lake fed by the natural springs that crossed the park flowing from the hills to the north.

PHIPPS CONSERVATORY. As a boy, Henry Phipps grew up within an easy walk of the commons. In 1888, the successful steel man contributed a spacious conservatory to the people of Allegheny City. Built near the site of the old penitentiary, the Phipps Conservatory became one of the most visited features of the Allegheny Park. Floral displays were maintained both within and without the collection of greenhouses.

MUSIC PAVILION. Shortly after the construction of the Phipps Conservatory, the parks commission contracted for the design and construction of a music pavilion to be placed near the conservatory. The design of architect James Madison Balph was selected. As the project was under construction, Balph died, and his partner, Andrew Peebles, completed the work.

HUMBOLDT MONUMENT. As a tribute to the great German scientist and philosopher Alexander von Humboldt, the Jefferson Masonic Lodge (a German-speaking lodge) of Allegheny arranged for the design and construction of the Humboldt Monument. The cornerstone was laid in place by an elaborate Masonic program on September 14, 1869. It was located in North Park across from Resaca Place.

HAMPTON BATTERY MONUMENT. On May 29, 1871, the Hampton Battery Monument was dedicated to the memory of Capt. Robert B. Hampton and other members of this famous light artillery battery whose lives were lost in the Civil War. The monument, placed in the East Park south of East Ohio Street, was erected by surviving members of the battery.

GEORGE WASHINGTON MONUMENT. This stunning granite monument, crafted by Edward Ludwig Pausch and honoring the first president, George Washington, was unveiled at an elaborate ceremony on February 23, 1891. This statue was commissioned by the Junior Order of United American Mechanics and placed in the North Park across from Sherman Avenue.

WASHINGTON MONUMENT MEDAL. Newspaper accounts of the unveiling ceremonies at the statue of Washington indicate that there were thousands of Alleghenians in attendance. To commemorate the event, a special medal was cast and given to all those who participated in the ceremonies.

THOMAS A. ARMSTRONG STATUE. In the late 19th century, the labor movement among the various crafts throughout the region was strong. One of the champions of labor was Thomas A. Armstrong. As a journalist, Armstrong stood squarely for the interests of working-class men and women. To honor Armstrong, labor groups from far and near raised funds for this monument placed in West Park near West Ohio Street.

SPANISH-AMERICAN WAR MEMORIAL. Friend W. Jenkins, a lieutenant in the U.S. Navy, was born in Allegheny. This naval officer was stationed on the USS *Maine* when it exploded in Havana in February 1898. In later years, the community raised funds to place a memorial in West Park to Jenkins and others who served in the Spanish-American War. The central feature was a portion of a torpedo tube from the destroyed ship.

SOUTH PARK FOUNTAIN. The southern section of the Allegheny Park was a narrow piece of property separating Stockton Avenue from North Canal Street and the rail line. Many of the city's fine old homes, along with the Allegheny Hospital, were located along Stockton, which, in earlier times, was part of the fashionable "Second Bank." The park commission authorized the placement of a handsome stone fountain there.

WEST PARK FOUNTAIN. The southwest section of West Park was bounded by Ridge and Irwin (Brighton Road) Avenues and West Ohio Street. Many of Allegheny City's wealthiest families lived in newly constructed mansions facing the park. In this rather quiet section of the park containing a large variety of trees, an elaborate fountain and pool were placed in a plaza setting surrounded by a ring of benches.

EAST PARK FOUNTAIN. When the leaders of Allegheny City decided to transform the common grazing land into a carefully designed urban park, they often referred to the space as the "lungs of the city." At a time when homes were fairly close to the industries along the rivers, and factories of various types were located in the midst of residential communities, the need for an open space was all the more desirable. Within the park, the Phipps Conservatory, the monuments and memorials, and the fountains were placed in locations that enhanced the design of the park itself. This was a park for walking, and a wide pathway, the promenade, ran through the center of East and North Parks. Where these pathways intersected at the northeast corner of the park, a great fountain and pool were placed. The image here is of the fountain and pool looking south at the promenade of East Park. The churches on the right are the First United Presbyterian of Allegheny and the Christ Episcopal. Both churches were located on Union Avenue.

ICE-SKATING. During the winter months, when Lake Elizabeth in Allegheny's West Park would freeze over, the youngsters (and oldsters too) would head to the park to ice-skate. This image, taken in the early 20th century, is of a winter day and a skating party on the lake that was surrounded by trees in the very heart of Allegheny City.

RIVERVIEW PARK KILBUCK RUN. In the 1890s, as the trolley lines were being extended to the city limits of Allegheny, a group of citizens raised funds to purchase the large tract of land in the Tenth Ward that became Riverview Park. While the parks in the heart of the city were more formal, Riverview Park had more of a natural setting. This pathway through a section of Riverview was called Kilbuck Run.

RIVERVIEW PARK. The topography of Riverview Park enabled the designers of the park to make effective use of valleys and hillsides. Where possible, pathways and steps were constructed through the woods and fields contained within the park's boundaries. Throughout the curved main roadway that was cut through the parkland, numerous entrances to the wooded trails were created, thereby allowing park users to enjoy the natural environment.

SPRINGHOUSE. The hilly terrain of Riverview Park contributed to the rivulets flowing through a number of wooded glades. At one particular location in the park, this vine-covered log springhouse was incorporated into the park design. It would have provided a welcome relief to hikers who used the walking and riding trails that wove through the hillsides.

ALLEGHENY OBSERVATORY. As the group of Allegheny's civic leaders was acquiring the property that would be given to the city for the creation of Riverview Park, there was a definite interest on the part of the Allegheny Observatory faculty and friends to relocate the observatory to a higher elevation. A two-acre site containing a high hilltop was adjacent to the parkland. This hill was privately purchased by David E. Parks, one of Allegheny's leading industrialists, and donated to the city as part of Riverview Park. The gift came with the stipulation that the crest of the hill would be used as the site for the construction of a new observatory. The architect selected to design the structure was Thorstein Billquist, and construction work began in 1900. When completed, the facility contained three telescopes, classrooms, laboratories, and lecture halls. It eventually became the final resting place of John Brashear and his wife, Phoebe.

NEW EXPOSITION BUILDINGS, EXPOSITION PARK ALLEGHENY CITY.

EXPOSITION HALL. The massive and ornately decorated Allegheny Tradesmen's Industrial Institute, known by most Alleghenians as Exposition Hall, was constructed to serve several purposes. First and foremost, it was used for trade shows where many products produced in the mills and factories of the region were exhibited. It was also used for social events. One such event, in October 1883, led to a massive fire that destroyed the entire structure.

BASEBALL AND HORSE RACING. Two of the sports interests in Allegheny City were baseball and horse racing. Exposition Park was developed as a baseball field for the Pittsburgh Pirates. Games of the first World Series between the Pirates and the Boston Red Sox were played in "Expo Park." Allegheny's horse racing track was on Brunot's Island. Spectators had to be ferried across to the island from the foot of Bayard (Branchport) Street in Manchester.

Eight

ALLEGHENIANS ALL

MARY ROBERTS RINEHART. In the opening lines of Gertrude Stein's autobiography, the author states that she was "firmly born" in Allegheny. Robinson Jeffers, Martha Graham, and Mary Cassatt could have made the same statement. Others, such as Andrew Carnegie, Henry Phipps, and the Oliver brothers, spent their formative years in Allegheny. However, to focus on the most recognized names results in telling only a small part of Allegheny's story. Mary Roberts Rinehart spent her childhood and much of her adult life in Allegheny City. Many of her novels focus on relationships and human behaviors that she observed in and about Allegheny City.

HENRY BUHL JR. A native of Butler County, Henry Buhl Jr. came to Allegheny City in the years following the Civil War and, with his business partner Russell H. Boggs, opened a small yard good store on Federal Street. Boggs and Buhl was to become the most fashionable department store in Allegheny City.

LOUISE BUHL. The Buhl home was located among a number of fashionable residences on Western Avenue. They had no children, but Louise Buhl was greatly involved with community groups that focused on the needs of children. Her husband frequently spoke of the generous nature of his wife and the impact she had on his own sense of giving back to the community.

RUSSELL HURD BOGGS. Like his partner Henry Buhl Jr., Russell H. Boggs came to Allegheny from the Evans City area in Butler County. Boggs was the president of their department store operation and was also married to Henry Buhl's sister. Their home was on West North Avenue across from the Allegheny Park. Along with his interest in the department store, Boggs was also a major owner of the Pittsburgh, Butler, Harmony, and New Castle Railway Company.

HARRY H. HIPWELL. One of the founders of the Hipwell Manufacturing Company, Harry Hipwell came to Allegheny City in the 1880s. He and his brother established a small factory on West North Avenue where they manufactured a variety of products from sheet metal. By the dawn of the 20th century, the Hipwell company was producing its major product, flashlights, for a nationwide market.

99

JAMES ALLEN DORSEY. In the 1890s, the family of James A. Dorsey resided on Alpine Street in the Second Ward of Allegheny City. Dorsey worked for George G. Splane, who owned and operated a drugstore in Pittsburgh, while his family grew up in Allegheny City and attended the Mary Junkin Cowley School on Palo Alto Street.

DAVID B. OLIVER
Capitalist and manufacturer
Interested in numerous large enterprises

DAVID BROWN OLIVER. The Oliver family came to Allegheny from Ulster in 1840. David B. Oliver and his brothers, Henry and James, were involved in the iron and steel industry from the late 1860s. In the early 1870s, David and his wife, Sarah Cunningham Oliver, moved to Allegheny City's Eleventh Ward. David served on the Allegheny School Board for many years. He was known as "the father of public education."

THOMAS HANNA. Through a very liberal bequest from Thomas Hanna and his son James, the Allegheny Seminary of the United Presbyterian Church was able to purchase property for the construction of a new seminary. In 1855, a lot at the corner of Buena Vista Street and West North Avenue was purchased by the denomination. In 1860, Hanna Hall was opened.

JOHN PARKE. A storyteller by nature, John Parke produced a history of Allegheny drawn from his own recollections. Parke was born in 1808 and came to live in Allegheny when his business ventures brought him to Manchester. He lived on Page Street in 1885. His recollections were collected and published in 1886.

JANE AND MATILDA SMITH. Two extremely benevolent daughters of Hugh and Charlotte Darsie Smith, Jane and Matilda Smith were born in the 1830s in Allegheny City. Their father was a successful coal merchant and steamboat operator. Their family also invested in the Crucible Steel Company. Following the death of their brother, these sisters contributed generously to the geology department of the Western University of Pennsylvania and to the Allegheny Observatory.

FREDERICK J. OSTERLING
Architect

FREDERICK J. OSTERLING. While he was at an early age, Frederick J. Osterling's teachers at Manchester School where he attended recognized his keen ability to draw and design. After leaving grade school, Osterling attended the Lessing Institute and then went abroad to further his architectural skills. Allegheny High School was one of many buildings in Allegheny designed by Osterling for clients in his own hometown.

MARGARET DELAND. Maple Grove was the name of the Bakewell estate that overlooked the village of Manchester and the Ohio River. It was here at Maple Grove that Margaret Deland grew up with the Bakewell and Campbell families. Several of Deland's works of fiction, *Old Chester Tales* and *Dr. Lavender's People*, are based on her recollections of village life in early Manchester.

Old Chester Tales

By

Margaret Deland

With Illustrations by

Howard Pyle

HARPER & BROTHERS PUBLISHERS
NEW YORK AND LONDON
1904

FR. SUITBERT G. MOLLINGER. On the day that the Most Holy Name of Jesus Church on Troy Hill was dedicated in 1868, Bishop Michael Domenec announced the appointment of Fr. Suitbert G. Mollinger to that parish. He served there until his death in 1892. While on Troy Hill, Mollinger paid for the construction of the church rectory as well as St. Anthony's Chapel, which contained the priest's private collection of relics.

103

ANDREW CARNEGIE. Born in the Scottish village of Dunfermline, Andrew Carnegie arrived in Allegheny City with his family in 1848. He is pictured here with his younger brother Tom. The story of Carnegie's rise to a position of great wealth and economic power became legendary in American history. Although Carnegie's early years in the steel industry occurred when living in Allegheny, by 1875 he had moved to New York City.

HENRY PHIPPS. From a small section of streets and alleys of Allegheny City's First Ward emerged several young men (Carnegie, Henry Phipps, and the Oliver brothers) who went on in life contributing to one another's great economic success. Phipps, after attaining considerable wealth in the steel industry, returned to the First Ward to build the Phipps Dwellings, designed to improve housing conditions for working-class families.

JOHN BRASHEAR. Although a native of Brownsville and a longtime resident of the South Side of Pittsburgh, John Brashear was drawn to Allegheny through his association with the Allegheny Observatory. Brashear was given financial support from William Thaw to establish a lens factory on Perrysville Avenue at the intersection with Buena Vista Street. For many years he took an active leadership role in the astronomy department at the Western University of Pennsylvania.

SAMUEL P. LANGLEY. Shortly after the Western University of Pennsylvania took over Allegheny Observatory, Prof. Samuel P. Langley was contracted as the head of the astronomy department. During his tenure at the observatory, Langley became internationally known for his many experiments in the field of aviation. Langley was often identified as the "father of aviation" because of his scientific breakthroughs achieved in Allegheny City.

GEORGE DAHNER. Among the many unsung heroes throughout Allegheny City were those men who staffed the fire stations. George Dahner became a firefighter in 1871. Dahner and his family lived on Perry (Phineas) Street in the heart of Allegheny City's Third Ward. He was assigned to Engine Company No. 2 located on Madison Avenue just around the corner from his home.

BENJAMIN F. WILLIAMS. In the early years of Allegheny City, its police station was located in a section of the city hall. With the growth in population, substations were established throughout the city and the ranks of the department were expanded. Patrolman Benjamin F. Williams, a resident of 828 Douglas (Doughton) Place, was one of "Allegheny's Finest" who kept order in the city's neighborhoods.

BENJ. F. WILLIAMS
Sub-Patrolman

GEORGE FERRIS. A native of Illinois and a graduate from the engineering school of Rensselaer, George Ferris came to Allegheny to work as a bridge designer and contractor. Ferris lived on Arch Street in the 1890s, when he designed the first Ferris wheel for the 1893 World's Columbian Exhibition in Chicago.

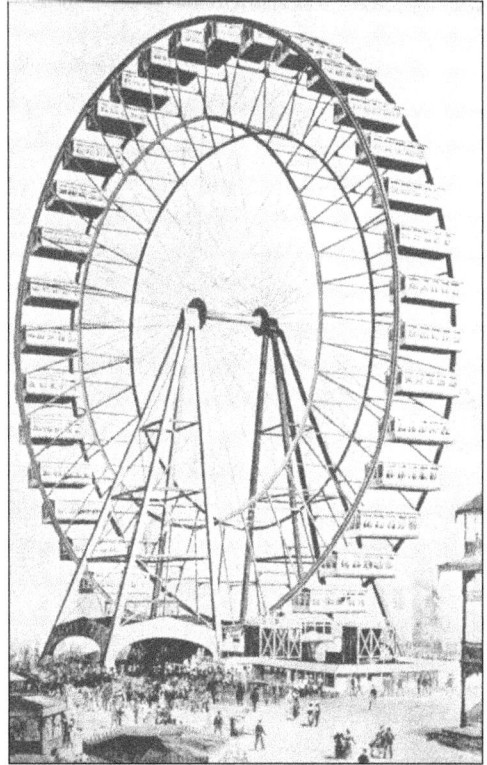

HENRY J. HEINZ. Even though Henry J. Heinz was not an Alleghenian by birth or residence, he was, however, an Alleghenian in spirit. At this picnic table are family and employees. Heinz, at the head of the table, looks out over family, including his son Howard at the front left, and employees such as Anna Shannon, a company secretary from Allegheny's Fourth Ward. Shannon is sitting fourth from the front on the right side of the table.

KATE DRUMMOND. One of the responsibilities of the Allegheny City Police Department was overseeing the operation of the city's jail. Kate Drummond was on the department staff as one of the matrons at the jail. In 1900, Drummond, who was a widow, resided on Linden Street in the Third Ward.

MRS. KATE DRUMMOND
Matron

GEORGE HASKO. Many of the Slovak families coming to Allegheny in the late 19th century settled close by the industrial sections of the city, the neighborhoods along the rivers. George Hasko immigrated as a young man. He eventually lived in the Spring Garden neighborhood, from which he walked to work at the Heinz factories. Hasko brought with him many of the customs of the Old World as he adapted to his life in the new.

Nine

THE GLORY YEARS
THEN ANNEXATION

THE ALLEGHENY POST OFFICE. In the last decade of the 19th century, Allegheny City was the third-largest city in Pennsylvania. Public buildings constructed in an earlier era were replaced with more impressive structures. Magnificent mansions were built on the street bordering the parks. Trolley lines connected the original four wards with Allegheny's new residential neighborhoods. Industries grew, resulting in more jobs for new immigrant groups. In 1897, a new post office building was constructed on West Ohio Street. However, behind the sense of progress and growth were whispers of consolidating Allegheny and Pittsburgh. By 1906, the whispers became speeches leading to an election and annexation.

MAP OF ALLEGHENY CITY, 1880. The geographic size of Allegheny City in 1880 was three times what it had been 40 years earlier. In 1848, there were just four wards; in 1898, that number had more than doubled. The city had become well connected with roadways, trolley lines, and

rail service. It was a strong and stable municipality. The social composition of the community was comparable to any major American city of the era.

ALLEGHENY CENTER. The four public squares at the center of the original plan for Allegheny Town continued to be public squares more than a century after the 1787 plan was conceived. The city hall, the Carnegie Free Library of Allegheny, and the Allegheny Market House occupied three squares. In the fourth square was Ober Park, a gift to the people of Allegheny by the civic-minded brewer.

THE ALLEGHENY MARKET. In an era when refrigeration was based on the regular delivery of ice, most people shopped daily. Every trolley line in the city made a stop near the Allegheny Market. Inside the market were stalls for butchers, green grocers, poultry dealers, dairymen, and trades people. Outside the market there were vendors selling all manner of goods.

112

CARNEGIE FREE LIBRARY OF ALLEGHENY. "Allegheny was my first love" was a comment attributed to Andrew Carnegie when he offered to the Allegheny City leaders a building to house a library, if they would agree to maintain both the building and the library. Included in the building complex was space for the library, a lecture hall, and a music hall. This image focuses on the entrance to the music hall from East Ohio Street.

INVITATION TO THE OPENING OF ALLEGHENY'S LIBRARY. The events, public and private, attending to the opening ceremonies of the Carnegie Free Library of Allegheny were quite extravagant. The official opening of the facility occurred on February 20, 1890. Carnegie was in attendance, along with Pres. Benjamin Harrison, who came from Washington to participate in this high-profile event.

ANDERSON MONUMENT. Early in 1898, Andrew Carnegie wrote to a friend, "I wish a monument erected to Col. Anderson to stand in front of the Allegheny." The monument was an act of appreciation by Carnegie to the generosity of James Anderson, who had opened his own library to working boys, including Carnegie. The Anderson Monument was located at the northeast corner of Federal and East Ohio Streets, adjacent to the entrance to the library building.

CARNEGIE LIBRARY INTERIOR. The public rooms in the interior of the Carnegie library were spacious and finely appointed. When the library opened, it was within walking distance of the Western University of Pennsylvania, three Presbyterian theological seminaries, and Allegheny High School. Students and scholars from these institutions placed a requirement on the library to maintain a well-stocked reference department.

FORT WAYNE RAILROAD STATION. In the early 1900s, the Pittsburgh, Fort Wayne, and Chicago rail system began a process of widening its right-of-way through Allegheny City. In the process, a new train station was built on Federal Street at the site of the former depot. At that time, the Fort Wayne Railroad Station in Allegheny was a major regional passenger and freight terminal.

INTERIOR, FORT WAYNE RAILROAD STATION. When the Fort Wayne Railroad Station was designed, the exterior of the building was done in a Flemish style. The interior, however, was very functional without much Victorian-era decoration. The use of skylights in the passenger waiting room gave additional light to an almost cavernous space.

115

GUM'S MEAT MARKET. Beyond the Allegheny City center, a growing number of small family-owned bakeries, meat markets, and grocery stores provided their products to the folks in the surrounding neighborhoods. The Gum family lived above its butcher shop located at the corner of Nelson (Nash) and Avery Streets.

D. HOLLANDER
THE POPULAR CLOTHIER, MERCHANT
TAILOR AND MEN'S OUTFITTER
413-415 OHIO STREET
ALLEGHENY

DAVID HOLLANDER. David Hollander, a native of Prussia, came to America in 1865. He settled in Allegheny City and established himself as a merchant tailor and clothier. By the 1890s, Hollander owned one of the largest clothing stores on East Ohio Street. This successful businessman resided on Avery Street and was a member of the Jefferson Lodge, Allegheny City's German Masonic fraternity, and the Concordia Club.

H. J. HEINZ COMPANY. Beginning in 1884, the H. J. Heinz Company began acquiring properties in the Eighth Ward of Allegheny City. By the 1890s, the company expanded food-processing operations to such an extent that its complex of buildings was its own industrial park. Located along River Road, the H. J. Heinz Company provided thousands of jobs for men and women, most of whom lived in the eastern neighborhoods of Allegheny.

H. J. HEINZ COMPANY KITCHENS. Henry J. Heinz, the food processor, was an ardent advocate of the Pure Food and Drug Acts. He not only sought to produce healthy food, but he sought to create a workplace in his kitchens and other departments that respected the dignity of his workforce. Heinz, unlike many industrial leaders of his era, worked to create safe and humane working conditions for all his employees.

RIDGE AVENUE. Time and travel considerations in the pre-automobile American urban culture resulted in people living a fairly short distance from where they worked. This was evident in housing patterns of the row houses in mill towns and in "millionaires' row" in major cities. The decade of the 1890s was the culmination of this pattern in Allegheny City. Ridge Avenue houses were homes of some of the wealthiest families in the region.

H. W. OLIVER HOUSE. Henry W. Oliver, the son of parents who arrived in Allegheny from Ulster, lived and worked in Allegheny during his formative years. Oliver and his brothers entered into the steel business at an early age. He was one among a few successful investors in acquiring vast tracts of land in the iron ore fields of Minnesota. He and his wife, Edith Cassidy Oliver, and their one daughter moved into this home on Ridge Avenue in 1879.

118

IRWIN AVENUE. The section of Irwin Avenue between Ridge and West North Avenues had an extraordinary location across from West Park. Several members of the B. F. Jones family had homes here in the 1890s. Among their neighbors were families of other steel barons. The arrival of the automobile in the early 20th century resulted in many of these families moving out of the city.

PAINTER HOUSE. The firm of Longfellow, Alden, and Harlow designed the Irwin Avenue residence of Augustus E. A. and Mary Blair Painter in 1887. The Painter family had been leaders in the iron and steel industry from its early years before the Civil War. When this home was built it was considered one of the most elaborate homes in Allegheny.

WESTMINSTER PRESBYTERIAN CHURCH. In the early 1890s, a massive new Presbyterian church was built in the Shadyside community of Pittsburgh. In those same years, a new congregation of Presbyterians gathered in Allegheny. This Westminster Presbyterian Church congregation agreed to the design of a church building smaller but similar to the Shadyside church. The historian James D. Van Trump pointed out that the design of the Shadyside church was much like Trinity Church designed by H. H. Richardson in Boston. This style featured a great auditorium space beneath a massive single tower. This "lantern" form was used by the Westminster congregation for its church building on Buena Vista Street.

SIXTH STREET BRIDGE. During the last half of the 19th century, remarkable strides were made in the field of science and its practical application. In the area of bridge building, the great engineer and inventor John Roebling developed a system of producing wire cable used in the construction of suspension bridges. Between 1858 and 1860, Roebling designed and oversaw the construction of the bridge crossing the Allegheny River from Federal Street.

NUNNERY HILL INCLINE. Another technological breakthrough of the same era was using wire cable in the operation of incline systems. The Nunnery Hill Incline, the area's first curved-track incline, operated from 1887 to 1899. This incline was very important to the development of the Nunnery Hill (Fineview) neighborhood. At one point there were four inclines in Allegheny City taking residents to new "hilltop" communities.

ENGINE COMPANY NO. 1. In communities having most structures consisting of frame buildings, the fear of fire was constant. Allegheny City, throughout its history, constructed many fine fire stations. As the city grew in size, so did the number of stations. Each fire station was extremely important to the neighborhood where it was located. Engine Company No. 1, the Hope Hose Company, was located on Martin (Martindale) Street.

ENGINE COMPANY NO. 14. As residential development expanded into Wards 10 and 11, the Allegheny City Fire Department established new fire companies and built more stations. One of the last stations to be built was Engine Company No. 14, which was located on Perrysville Avenue just beyond the East Street intersection.

122

FLOOD SCENE, FEDERAL STREET. The year 1907 was not a good year in the minds of many Alleghenians. On March 15, the city neighborhoods along the banks of the Allegheny and Ohio Rivers experienced a widespread flood. The business district of the lower sections of Federal Street was covered with water as high as the first floor of some homes and shops.

FLOOD SCENE, EXPOSITION PARK. The floodwaters that devastated many families along the Allegheny River floodplain also swept across all of Exposition Park. Positive memories of the World Series that was played there in 1903 were replaced by images of mud and water and the debris left on the field when the waters finally receded.

CHARLES FREDERICK KIRSCHLER. A widely known businessman, banker, and political leader from Allegheny City's Fifth Ward, Charles F. Kirschler assumed the office of mayor of Allegheny City in 1906. He was the last mayor of the city. During Kirschler's brief tenure, the Pennsylvania legislature, with strong urging from Gov. Samuel W. Pennypacker, enacted the Greater Pittsburgh Act that set the stage for the consolidation of Allegheny City and Pittsburgh. On June 12, 1906, a special election was held in both cities with the total results favoring consolidation. Many Alleghenians who opposed the forced annexation challenged the legitimacy of the Greater Pittsburgh Act in both state and federal courts. The final decision issued from the Supreme Court of the United States on Friday, December 6, 1907, affirmed the Greater Pittsburgh Act, thus paving the way for immediate consolidation. The following Monday, December 9, 1906, Charles F. Kirschler was sworn in as deputy mayor of the city of Pittsburgh.

124

MEETING OF ALLEGHENY CITY AND PITTSBURGH POLITICAL LEADERS. Monday, December 9, 1906, was a bright day for those who advocated for Pittsburgh's annexation of Allegheny City. For many citizens on the north side of the river it was indeed a dark day. In the months between the election of June 12, 1906, and the ruling of the Supreme Court on December 7, 1907, political leaders in both cities began planning for what seem to become the inevitable. There was a determination to make the process of annexation as smooth as possible if the court rulings favored annexation. On that Monday morning, the political leaders as well as department heads met in the city hall of Pittsburgh to establish how a Greater Pittsburgh would function. Allegheny's mayor, Charles F. Kirschler, became Pittsburgh's deputy mayor. Many other Allegheny City officials, such as Edward Lang and Robert Swan, were appointed to key positions in the new administration. It would be many, many years, however, before a resident of the North Side would be elected mayor of the city of Pittsburgh.

THE MARRIAGE OF MISS ALLEGHENY AND PA PITT. The Greater Pittsburgh Act that resulted in the "marriage of Allegheny and Pittsburgh" was written in a manner that gave the advantage to the citizens of Pittsburgh. Rather than requiring that a majority of the voters in both cities was necessary to bring about a consolidation, the bill required that a majority of all the votes cast would settle the issue. The election results on the issue of consolidation in Allegheny were 6,570 in favor and 12,005 opposed; the results in Pittsburgh were 31,116 in favor and 5,430 opposed. The total votes were 37,686 in favor and 17,435 opposed. After an 18-month battle in the courts, the marriage went off as the governor and legislature had planned.

BIBLIOGRAPHY

Allegheny County—A Sesqui-centennial Review. Pittsburgh: Allegheny Sesqui-centennial Committee, 1938.

Art Work of Pittsburg. Chicago: W. H. Parish Publishing Company, 1893.

The Art Work of Pittsburg. George E. White Company, 1899.

Brown, Eliza Smith. *In Pursuit of Breathing Place: A History of the Allegheny Commons.* Brown, Carlisle and Associates, 1996.

Copeland, Robert M. *Spare No Exceptions: 175 Years of the Reformed Presbyterian Theological Seminary.* Pittsburgh: Reformed Presbyterian Theological Seminary, 1986.

Deland, Margaret. *Old Chester Tales.* New York and London: Harper and Brothers, 1904.

Glenn, Monsignor Francis A. *Shepherds of the Faith 1843–1993.* Pittsburgh: Diocese of Pittsburgh, 1993.

History and Institutions—City of Allegheny, PA. Allegheny City, PA: Allegheny Evening Record, 1896.

History of Allegheny Police Department. Allegheny, PA: Patrolmen's Benevolent Association, 1901.

History of the Allegheny Fire Department. John P. Shay, 1907.

Kidney, Walter C. *Pittsburgh Landmark Architecture.* Pittsburgh: Pittsburgh History and Landmarks Foundation, 1997.

Lee, R. H. *The Life of Harriet Preble.* Press of Henry B. Ashmead, 1876.

Maszkiewicz, Ruth C. *The Presbyterian Hospital of Pittsburgh.* Pittsburgh: Presbyterian Hospital, 1997.

Palmer, R. M. *Palmer's Pittsburgh—Past and Present.* Pittsburgh: 1905.

Pittsburg at the Dawn of the 20th Century. Pittsburgh: Pittsburg Leader, 1901.

Sheatsley, C. V. *A Brief History of St. John's Evangelical Lutheran Church.* Pittsburgh: C. M. Rodgers Company, 1913.

Souvenir of Pittsburgh and Allegheny City, PA. Columbus, OH: Ward Brothers, 1887.

Spatz, Richard E. *The History of Allegheny Country Club.* Sewickley, PA: Urbina Publishing, 1995.

St. Boniface Parish Centennial 1884–1994. New Kensington, PA: Beacon Printing Company Inc., 1984

Wittemann, A. *Pittsburgh and Allegheny.* New York: Albertype Company, 1891.

Visit us at
arcadiapublishing.com

www.ingramcontent.com/pod-product-compliance
Lightning Source LLC
Chambersburg PA
CBHW080547110426
42813CB00006B/1242